DO IT

FOREWORD BY
MEL ROBBINS

THE
**LIFE-CHANGING
POWER**
OF
TAKING ACTION

DO
IT

DAVID NURSE

WILEY

Published by John Wiley & Sons, Inc., Hoboken, New Jersey.
Published simultaneously in Canada.

For general information on our other products and services or for technical support, please
contact our Customer Care Department within the United States at (800) 762-2974, outside
the United States at (317) 572-3993 or fax (317) 572-4002.

Wiley also publishes its books in a variety of electronic formats. Some content that appears in
print may not be available in electronic formats. For more information about Wiley products,
visit our web site at www.wiley.com.

Library of Congress Cataloging-in-Publication Data is Available:

ISBN 9781119853701 (Hardback)
ISBN 9781119853763 (ePDF)
ISBN 9781119853756 (ePub)

Cover Design: Paul McCarthy
Cover Photo: Courtesy of the Author

SKY10042568_020823

To my wife, Taylor. Without you I wouldn't be the person I am today. You are my heartbeat; you are my soul.

To God. You are the reason I do what I do. All glory and honor to Your Kingdom!

To my future kids. When you read this book, I hope you go for your dreams. Don't let anyone tell you that you can't do something. Your mom and I love you so much and we believe in you!

CONTENTS

FOREWORD

You made a smart choice when you picked up this book.

I bet you picked up this book because there's something about your life that you want to change. Maybe life is kicking you in the ass so you have no choice but to change.

Yet as bad as you want it, you can't seem to flip the channel and make it happen.

You might even feel so paralyzed that you can't get from thought to action.

For a very long time, that was me.

In 2008, I nearly destroyed my marriage, my family, and my career because I couldn't move. I waited to feel motivated. It took me hitting rock bottom personally and financially to finally discover the secret to hacking motivation.

Once I did, it changed my life. And once you learn it, I know it will change yours, too.

So let me back up a little.

I was 41 years old, with three kids under the age of ten, living outside of Boston. Though trained as a lawyer, I stopped practicing once we moved from New York and instead had what felt like a solid job working with a tech start-up.

My husband and his best friend had followed their dream of opening a pizza restaurant. With their first location a booming success, they decided to open another. Because we were certain the second store would be just as successful, we cashed out our life savings and took out a home equity line to pay for the expansion. I mean, what could go wrong?

Actually, everything.

Later that year, the housing market tanked and the country was driven into a financial crisis. The second restaurant crashed, taking our entire savings with it. On top of that, I lost my job, the liens started hitting the house, and bankruptcy letters came flooding in.

I took out all my frustration on Chris, so our marriage was hanging by a thread. We both numbed the pain with alcohol, and many nights I ended the day by passing out on the couch.

My kids were getting themselves off to school most mornings. And when they didn't, I had to drive them in late.

I couldn't do anything. I felt paralyzed. Caught in a mental loop that repeated what a failure I was. Failed as a wife. Failed as a lawyer. Failed as a mother. Failed at life.

Rationally, I knew that it would help if I looked for a job. I knew I could call my parents and ask for help. I knew I should reach out to friends. I knew I should exercise. I knew I shouldn't drink so much. I knew I should be nicer to Chris because he was doing everything he could.

And on and on and on. Point is, I KNEW what to do.

And yet, I didn't do any of those things. Why? Because I didn't feel motivated. I didn't want to.

I felt depressed. Anxious. Angry. Scared. But never did I feel motivated to do what I had to do to change the situation we were in.

So it was on one of those nights, when I was nearly passed out on the couch after one too many Manhattans, that it happened.

The TV is on while I'm giving myself this award-winning drunken pep talk:

All right, that's it, Mel. Tomorrow morning, woman. It's the new you tomorrow morning.

You have to look for a new job.

You have to stop drinking so much.

You have to call your parents and ask for help.

You have to call the creditors.

You have to stop screaming at Chris.

And by God, woman, when that alarm clock goes off, you cannot hit that snooze button five times.

You cannot lay there like a human pot roast marinating in fear.

You, woman, are gonna get outta bed and get those kids on that bus.

Now, I'm not sure if it was fate, but what happened next changed the trajectory of my life.

Out of the corner of my eye, on the TV, I see a rocket ship about to take off at the end of a commercial. Then it's the countdown: 5 . . . 4 . . . 3 . . . 2 . . .1 . . . and the engines power up and flames are everywhere and there goes the rocket, shooting up toward space!

And it hits me.

That was it! That was the answer to getting up the next morning when that alarm clock went off. I was going to count down and launch myself out of bed.

For whatever reason, that visual of the rocket gave me hope for the next day.

And that hope was my spark.

So alarm rings the next morning and . . . I hit the snooze.

But then I remembered that rocket. And my promise.

Here's the thing about hesitation, which has taken me years of research to understand. There is a five-second window that defines your whole life.

This five-second window will determine how much money you make, how happy you are, how fulfilling your relationships are, and how purposeful you feel.

Because it's in that five-second window between a thought you have and the action you either take or don't take that a chain of events is set off.

And as soon as you hesitate, you give your brain the chance it needs to start making up excuses about why you can't do something.

That's when anxiety, fear, and imposter syndrome hijack your life.

Though I didn't know all of the research that morning after the rocket ship, I did remember the promise I made to myself. So as soon as I hit the snooze, instead of burying myself back under the covers of my bed, I started to count back.

5 . . . 4 . . . 3 . . . 2 . . . 1 . . .

And I got myself out of bed.

That day the kids made it to school on time.

And over the course of the next few months, creditors were called, appointments with the bank were made, and my husband and I started to have conversations again.

It wasn't perfect, but one action at a time, we started to dig ourselves out from the dark hall we'd fallen into.

And that's what this book is about to teach you. I can't wait to see where it takes you.

You are one decision away from a different life, a better life, this book will ignite that fire inside of you and replace fear with action.

xo, Mel Robbins

—Host of the number-one-ranking The Mel Robbins Podcast and
New York Times–bestselling author of *The High 5 Habit*
and *The 5 Second Rule*

INTRODUCTION

Action. A relatively small word that demands effort and breeds better. Yet, nothing about it feels small. Nor should it. When it comes to dreams and goals, *action* is the biggest word of them all. And let's face it, big can be complicated, intimidating, and scary. Trust me, if anyone gets it, it's me. I've been there before. In that same boat you are in as you read this book. Afraid of action. Afraid of failure. Afraid of a lot of things.

"David, see me outside when you're done in the locker room," my coach hollered before returning on court to answer questions from the media.

I just finished playing in my first *real* game of professional basketball in Spain. I'd always dreamt of playing in the NBA, and I'd be lying if I didn't tell you that I'd also always dreamt of playing basketball professionally in Spain. My older sister studied in Spain for two years during which I vicariously lived through her stories and photos. I wrote about Spanish life and business for my 50-page capstone project in college. Even as a child, I made my family stop to eat tapas at the Spain booth in Disney's Epcot International Food and Wine Festival every time we vacationed there. (My dad is a Disney fanatic, so much so that my parents even honeymooned there. So, naturally 99% of my childhood vacations consisted of Disney.) All this to say, I knew I was meant to be in Spain. And I especially knew that I was meant to be playing basketball. This was the closest steppingstone I had to the NBA.

As I waited outside the locker room, I took in the brisk early fall evening. The backdrop of the Basque Mountains lining the Northern Iberian Peninsula was like a picturesque painting. The breeze coming off the Cantabrian Sea blew in my hair, adding the refreshing touch I needed after a hard-fought game.

I felt good, *really* good. I was meant to be here; I just knew it in my bones.

"David," coach called out as he motioned for me to join him on the opposite side of the street.

"Walk with me."

I figured he would tell me he had selected me to be the captain of the team, to be the on-court extension of himself: the player-coach essentially.

But when his next words hit my ears, I suddenly wished that I could "no comprendo." But I understood; I understood far too well.

"We're going to have to send you home," he said with a look that melded stern and disdain together. "I don't think you are going to be able to cut it."

My heart sank.

My body sank.

I tried to hold it together, but inside I was crumbling.

Without any more explanation, the head coach disclosed they would have a car waiting out front in the morning to take me to the airport with a one-way ticket home to Kansas City.

And just like that, it was over.

Gone.

All my hopes, goals, and dreams washed away in a single breath from a coach I thought was my friend.

Oh, how quickly the tides can turn.

I don't remember much of the 14+ hour flight home. I must have sat there staring out the window the entire time in total shock. But, as I wandered off the plane in Kansas City, I felt as if I was in a scene from a movie. You know, the one where everything is happening around the main character in real time while they're in zombie land unable to hear anything but the thoughts screaming in their head.

That was me. And not just as I slugged off the plane, but for the next *six months*.

My body physically went through the motions of life, but my mind, my heart, and my soul were almost completely absent. I was one-tenth present, nine-tenths broken.

And I had no idea how to move on.

I waited for the phone to ring. Surely my agent would secure another job for me to play professionally overseas.

But the phone never rang.

I waited for my parents to make everything okay and have a job lined up for me so I could earn some money and get a place of my own.

But that conversation never happened.

I waited for an email to come in from my college, Western Illinois University, where I had received my MBA just a few years prior. After all, the dean had said they would always take care of alumni. But an email like that never entered by inbox. And trust me, I checked the spam. Daily.

I was alone, on my own. No one teaches you what to do when all of your goals in life, everything you've prepared for, the thing you've poured every waking hour into is taken away in the blink of an eye without a lifeline in sight. No one teaches you how to make things happen. I was taught to wait until I was offered something: until the phone rang with an opportunity, until an email came in with a job offer. No one ever taught me how to take the reins of life into my own hands, let alone told me I'd need to.

I spent months living as if I were in a dark room with no light switch, moping around my parent's living room and laying back in their recliner chair (which became my room and my bed all in one). I listened to the early morning cacophony of my mom clunking and clanking dishes in the kitchen ten feet from my place of slumber on repeat.

At first, it was annoying but soon enough I learned to tune it out. I learned to tune out a lot.

"David . . . David . . . DAVID!" the voice increased from the kitchen until it bordered a yell loud enough to be heard throughout the neighborhood.

My mom had my attention.

I let my head plop toward her direction to acknowledge her but, more importantly, to signal that I had zero plans to decolonize from my recliner.

"You know what, David, life is funny. Just when you think you have it all, life hits you like an avalanche and takes it all away," my mom said without breaking stride as she placed dishes in the cupboard.

What the hell is she talking about, I thought.

My mom continued, "It's funny because just when you think a door is closed on life, it's actually not. The closed door allows other ones to open up so better opportunities can emerge. David, when one door closes, four open, and an entire beachfront patio overlooking the ocean."

What? I played it back in my mind as my mom exited the kitchen.

One door closes, and four open? That couldn't be right. I always thought it was one door closes, *one* more opens. And what's with the beachfront patio overlooking the ocean? Where was that coming from?

Something struck a chord. I was interested. More than interested, I was deeply intrigued.

So, if one door closes, my life isn't over?

If my goals of playing professional basketball are taken away from me, and another door in that same pursuit doesn't open, my life doesn't end?

Aren't I supposed to wait until the next door opens?

After settling in for bed that night (on the recliner, obviously), my mind couldn't stop racing. I was unable to shake the feeling that maybe there was actually something to what my mom said.

Maybe, just maybe, this mom-ism held valuable weight.

Since the door closed on basketball in Spain, maybe I don't have to wait around until another door opens. Maybe I don't have to let life just "happen to me." What if I can take the reins? What if my future is waiting for *me* to take action?

Was I sleep-deprived?

Was I dreaming?

When I woke up the next morning, the same thought sprung around my mind, pounding on each side of my brain begging to escape. I knew this moment was different. I knew that my mom's words, the ones I typically would have let go in one ear and out the other, had changed the trajectory of my life.

For the first time, I decided to give myself permission to allow the past to be what it was, *the past*.

I gave myself permission to expand my identity. No longer did I have to identify as strictly a "basketball player." I could funnel the shooting skills I had mastered as a player and my desire to make an impact in the basketball world through an entirely different door: adding the new identity of "basketball coach" to my repertoire.

I gave myself permission to not wait for life to be handed to me on a silver platter and instead decided from that point on to go get what I want.

I gave myself permission to *take action*.

I jumped out of the recliner, marched over to the printer, and grabbed every sheet of paper out of the tray. I began to write. And write. And write.

I composed a handwritten letter addressed to every NBA general manager in the league that introduced myself, expressed how much

I respected their organization, and stated that if there was anything I could do to serve them, I was all in.

What had gotten into me?

I went from a *victim* of life to the captain's seat.

Now, I could take you step-by-step through everything I did from that day on that led me to becoming an NBA coach. (Yes, I did accomplish it. Special shoutout to the *one* general manager who responded to my letter: the GM of the Los Angeles Clippers at the time, Gary Sacks. Every NBA connection and relationship I have to this day stems from Gary.)

But that's not the point.

The point is I began taking action in my life. *That* is the most important step.

I made the shift from allowing life to *happen to me*, to making life *happen for me*.

This book will introduce you to the different Action Archetypes. The main reasons why people don't take action in their life. There are nine of them to be exact.

1. The allodaxophobic
2. The burned
3. The inopportune
4. The blamer
5. The test-believer
6. The perfectionist
7. The scarciest
8. The distracted
9. The underestimater

At least one, maybe several, archetypes will immediately resonate with you. But at some point in your life, odds are you have (or will have) experienced each of them. I know I have. I see myself in every single one of the nine archetypes.

To develop these nine archetypes, I performed an extensive study: The Action Archetype Examination. I surveyed 3,100 people throughout the world. I chose people from all different types of social statuses, upbringings, and belief systems; the goal was to figure out the main roadblocks responsible for preventing people from taking action in their life. It is the most extensive *action* study conducted that I know of to date.

In this book, you will get clear intel on why your brain and your heart hold you back from taking action. You will learn how to turn what was once a blinding roadblock for you into a springboard for your success. And, in addition to understanding your own Action Archetype, you will gain insight into other people's behavior as well. Even if you resonate with only *one* archetype, the knowledge and understanding of each type will help you immensely to know why people act the way they do. This awareness will increase your effectiveness in the workplace and help you be a better spouse, a better parent, a better friend, a better *you*.

But I also must warn you, there is a common denominator that's dark and very real. It's not pretty and we all love to run from it.

Every single Action Archetype is rooted in a four-letter word: *fear*.

At some level, you have experienced the debilitating belief that if you take action, you will fail. So the obvious question is: Why take action at all?

Faith and fear both require you to believe in something you can't see.

But if faith and fear take the same amount of energy, why not choose faith over fear?

Easier said than done, I know.

Eight percent: that is the percentage of people who fulfill their dreams.

That means 92% do not.

That's it—8% of people live out their entire life on this earth doing what they love to do. The average amount of hours a human being lives on this earth is 692,040 hours. That's not a whole lot in the grand scheme of things.

So the question you need to ask yourself is this: Do you love what you do? Do you honestly, wholeheartedly, *love* what you do?

Notice I didn't ask if your life is bad. It's probably not! My life wasn't necessarily "horrible." But I was far from being fulfilled—I knew there was more. I was dancing with a mid-life malaise and I wasn't even in my mid-life yet. Sometimes you don't even know things could be better. All you know is all you know.

Fear will never *fully* go away. It's a part of life. But the difference in being paralyzed by fear versus viewing fear as an exciting adventure makes all the difference. Let me repeat that: it makes *all* the difference.

Commit to reading this book from front to back and I promise that when you are finished, you will be able to identify the exact roadblocks that keep you from taking action. When you finish this book, you will have the tools necessary to overcome your personal resistance, to navigate any roadblocks that stand in your way, and to break free of the chains keeping you from living a life of fulfillment.

At the end of the day, we are all searching for happiness. The only way to find happiness is by living a life of fulfillment. And the only way to achieve fulfillment is by taking action in your life.

Taking action = living a life of fulfillment = happiness.

Remember, you don't have to be great to start, but today you can start to be great. The choice is yours . . .

The Importance of History

We can learn a lot from history: the ones who have paved the way before us. In this book, you will learn about nine truly incredible people who overcame the same roadblocks that are holding you back now. People who changed the world despite being fearful of taking action. People who initially lived their life as one of the nine archetypes. People who overcame these fears and their archetype to eventually achieve a life of fulfillment. If they hadn't done so, the world we know today would look drastically different.

I could list off all the great things they accomplished and the obstacles they overcame but I would much rather you *feel* what it was like to be in their mind. So, you will take a front-row seat alongside each person as they embark on their journey. In doing so, you can observe and study what these experts did and use them as a guide for taking your own first step toward action.

Each chapter highlights one historical figure and how their riveting story relates to their specific Action Archetype. Each story covers four major plot points:

- Meet the person: a look into their life and the circumstances that led up to their looming decision

- The crux: the suspenseful moment when they come face-to-face with the decision to take action or not.

- What actually happened: the aftermath of that decision and how it altered their destiny

- Flip the script: what the world might look like today if they hadn't overcome their roadblock and taken action.

The Importance of Science

Action is not only backed by psychology; it is also woven through our physiology.

In each Action Archetype, you will learn from a neurological perspective about the brain and how it functions in regard to taking action (or not). We will also investigate the heart, aka your emotions, and why the heart plays a major role in whether or not you take action. The brain and the heart are two of the most vital driving forces in your daily decisions. By understanding how they function on a deeper level, you can use them for your benefit and prevent them from unknowingly holding you back.

The Brain

Our brain has three decision-making areas:

- The frontal cortex is responsible for deliberate decision-making.
- The motor cortex is responsible for movements that accompany decisions.
- The supplementary motor cortex is responsible for subconscious instincts.

In each decision we face, we have an option of activating any of these three areas of the brain. You use the frontal cortex when deciding on what you want to eat for dinner at a new restaurant, you rely on the motor cortex when you step up to bat and are deciding whether or not to swing at the 95 mph fastball hurling your way, and you rely on your supplementary motor cortex to steer your arm in the correct way to open a door. (I encourage you to look online for images of the brain and where these areas are located.)

If you hesitate while using the frontal cortex, you will probably be okay. But if you hesitate when using the motor cortex, you're stopped dead in your tracks.

So the question now is, how do you activate the supplementary motor cortex (SMA) so you can trust your instincts without hesitation when the 95 mph fastballs of life are hurling your direction?

The answer: there is no correct answer. Sure, there are ways to develop the SMA, like practicing reactionary drills with visual cues. But the answer no one wants to hear is the cold hard truth:

Repetition (daily habits) + Instinct (your gut feeling) + Trust (belief in the process) = Eliminating hesitation

Eliminating hesitation is needed to defeat fear and take action. If you hesitate in the boardroom, your question goes unasked. If you hesitate on stage speaking, you lose the trust of the audience. If you hesitate on the court before you shoot, you will more than likely miss. There is just 0.01 second that separates the greatest performers in the world from the thousands of good performers.

The Heart

For many years doctors and psychologists held firm that emotions were purely generated from the brain. However, in recent years this once widely agreed-on truth has been debunked. We know emotions can be contained in different organs throughout the body. The main organ responsible for emotion is none other than the heart. The heart is your *emotional brain.*

Studies conducted by the HeartMath Institute have shown a critical link between the heart and the brain. They are interconnected in a way that makes the heart and brain unable to function without each other. The heart sends signals and rhythm patterns to the brain. For example, when you experience feelings of stress, anxiety, worry, or anger, your heart's rhythm becomes erratic, signaling to the brain that there is something wrong. In response, the emotional centers in the brain become activated. This creates the feelings you experience in and around your heart.

The heart is your armor; it wants to protect you at all times.

The brain is your sword.

Together, working as one unit, this is what makes you a warrior: the brain and heart connection.

Brain and Heart Connection

Within each chapter, I will break down how the brain and the heart operate within each given Action Archetype. Although these sections are rooted in science and based on multitudes of studies, it is not meant to be an academic research dissertation. This book is meant to be a handbook that will help you identify roadblocks in your life and provide easy-to-apply tools that will ignite action.

Think of me as your *tour guide to action*. If I do my job, you will understand yourself and others more deeply. You will break through the roadblocks that have been holding you back. And, you will learn to thrive regardless of any obstacles, despite living in a society that encourages living in fear.

You can be in the 8% that accomplishes your dreams. You truly can DO IT.

DISCOVER YOUR ACTION ANIMAL

Are you like a meerkat, squirrel, or maybe a hippo? Maybe the echidna, a thoroughbred racehorse, or the butterfly speak to you. Each Action Archetype throughout this book is tied to an action animal.

Every animal has an incredibly unique role in society. Just like you. Animals function on instinct. Most people think animals are only concerned with *survival*. Well, most people are wrong. Animals are *thriving* species that don't live reactively but proactively. Just like you will learn to do.

We can learn a lot from our furry, feathery, scaly friends.

Animals don't worry about what their peers think of them.

Animals don't blame their parents, who gave them life.

Animals don't hold grudges toward another animal who stole their food three years ago.

Animals don't believe everything is scarce; even if it means flying 25 miles to find food, they know they will be fed.

Animals don't stress about perfectionism; they take action.

Animals don't underestimate themselves; the tiny common ant can lift 5,000 times its body weight!

Animals aren't worried if they are too young or too old, they impact their society from the day they are born until they day they die.

Animals don't take personality tests; they are genuinely who they are. A walrus isn't trying to fly like an eagle just because it was born in the month of January.

Animals aren't distracted by their surroundings; they have an ability to laser focus that makes the top athletes in the world jealous.

Be prideful of the animal you associate with. At heart we are all animals.

It's time to unleash your action animal!

And on that note, let's swing into action!

"Action is the antidote to despair."

—Joan Baez

"No one builds a legacy by standing still."

—Oscar Auliq-Ice

"The value of an idea lies in the using of it."

—Thomas Edison

"Be the change that you wish to see in the world."

—Mahatma Gandhi

"If you can't fly then run, if you can't run then walk, if you can't walk then crawl, but whatever you do you have to keep moving forward."

—Dr. Martin Luther King Jr.

"I never lose. Either I win or learn."

—Nelson Mandela

"There is nothing impossible to him who will try."

—Alexander the Great

"The best time to plant a tree was 20 years ago. The second best time is now."

—Chinese Proverb

"Do you want to know who you are? Don't ask. Act! Action will delineate and define you."

—Thomas Jefferson

"A superior man is modest in his speech, but exceeds in his actions."

—Confucius

"Thoughts do more. Words do much. Actions do much more."

—Israelmore Ayivor

"A journey of a thousand miles begins with a single step."

—Lao Tzu

"Impossible is just an opinion."

—Paulo Coelho

"Some people want it to happen, some wish it would happen, others make it happen."

—Michael Jordan

"Just Do It."

—Nike

"The best way to get out of anything is to do something. Something at least moves you somewhere . . ."

—Me . . . and after you read this book: YOU!

CHAPTER 1

The Allodoxaphobic

MEET MARTHA GRAHAM

Everything about it was out of the norm. Untamed and unrefined, yet rhythmic and sensual. Every arc, limb, and movement flowed with new energy, new breath. An explosion of expression through physical art, unlike anything Martha had ever seen.

Tucked in a back row of Los Angeles's Mason Opera House, 16-year-old Martha watched in awe as the barefoot dancers commanded the stage with power and passion.

"What is this?" she asked her father.

"It's Ruth St. Denis, dear," her father answered, eyes fixed on the stage.

It was 1911 and the only dance Martha had seen before this was classical ballet. Clean lines and graceful twirls she knew, but this was different. A form of dance with Mexican and Egyptian roots that refused to play by the rules.

Hooked, Martha turned to her father and proclaimed, "I'm going to be a dancer just like this someday." He smirked, attributing the comment to childlike wishful thinking. But Martha was filled with new-found certainty. She couldn't wait to get home to their Santa Barbara estate to tell her mom.

"Won't mother be so proud!" Martha thought. "I'll go on to change the world!" To her dismay, Martha's exuberance was not shared by her parents when she returned home.

"Dance is not a career, darling. It's a recreation for drunk peasants," her mother said dismissively. "You will stay put with us until you marry a wealthy young man who can provide for you and your family."

In an instant, Martha's dream began to crumble. Without her parents' support, becoming a dancer would be a fruitless endeavor. After all, their opinions mattered and without their encouragement and aid, Martha knew her pursuit would be exponentially more difficult. Defeated, Martha shoved her young dream to the shadows of her heart.

But the dream persisted, burning brighter every day, demanding attention. Try as she might, Martha knew there was no letting go. Ruth St. Denis had opened her eyes to a brand-new world and Martha was eager to explore its marvels.

She shared her dream with friends and the wonder she saw on stage that evening. Her friends didn't share her vision. Not only did they reject the notion, they ostracized her for thinking such fairytale thoughts.

One afternoon in her Santa Barbara schoolyard, Martha felt a strange sensation build within her. A rhythm only she could hear and a story only her body could tell. As the golden sun rained over her, Martha began to dance just as she had seen on the Mason Opera House stage. It was freeing and intoxicating. Self-expression like she had never experienced before. She was a natural. With her hair blowing in the wind and arms flailing with reckless beautiful abandon, her body moved to a beat that didn't sit well with those who passed by the schoolyard.

"Simp!"

"Ding-bat!"

"Need directions to the loony bin?!"

The insults shook Martha's wobbly confidence and as quickly as she discovered her dream for dance, the reality became joltingly clear. Sobbing, she ran home to tell her parents what happened.

"And that is precisely why we don't dance, Martha. Dancing is for the lower class; we are Grahams, not countrymen." Her mother's words stuck with her. "What have I been thinking?" Martha lamented. "I will never become a dancer. Not me. No way." Martha packed her dreams away once again and pushed them deep down inside of her, in fear of what others would think of her if she dared ever let them back out.

For the next five years, Martha tiptoed through life, going through the motions, doing what she was told, living the life her parents and friends wanted for her. Anything to avoid the scorn of others' disapproval. She chose to play it safe, knowing safe would always be accepted. However, the voice inside her would not be muted that easily.

One night, when Martha was in her early twenties, she had a vivid dream that pulled her from the theatre wings onto the stage, showing her a glimpse of the groundbreaking performer she could become. "Dance is an art form," a voice spoke out, hidden behind the harsh glare of the spotlight. "Martha, don't you see . . . you were meant to change the world."

When she woke up, Martha knew what she had to do, despite the fearful voice in her head. Trembling as she walked down the stairs to the kitchen table, Martha shared her dream with her parents, interpreting aloud her true calling.

"Ridiculous," her mother shouted. "Dreams are dreams for a reason. They're not real. Snap out of it, Martha!"

But she couldn't. She had to see her dream through. With newfound resolve, Martha announced she was leaving home and enrolling to study dance at The Denishawn School of Dancing in Los Angeles, created by none other than Ruth St. Denis and her husband Ted Shawn.

But leaving home was just the first of hurdles to come. In her early twenties, Martha was an outcast at dance school. She was a mere 5'2", not classically beautiful, and much older than the other dancers. Then, on the eve of her first performance, she had a surprise visitor: her mother. Martha's excitement quickly morphed to disdain.

"Martha, come home. Stop doing this to yourself and our family. We're worried about you. Your father and I will find you a nice husband who can support you. You don't have to do this. Stop now before you embarrass yourself."

Torn by her mother's opinion, Martha questioned if she could go on. Maybe her mother was right; maybe she should return home and give up. After all, the audience could very well laugh and mock her like her peers did back in the day. Was her dream really worth it? Why not just live the acceptable, easy life already set up for her?

"No, mother. I must stay. It is my destiny."

After much back-and-forth, her mother angrily left with the warning to never return home.

From the moment the lights went on, Ruth St. Denis could sense something was off. This wasn't the same dancer she had seen work tirelessly day in and day out, shielding off the input of those around her. She pulled Martha aside after the performance, and Martha began sobbing with her head in her hands.

"What's wrong, child?" Ruth asked with a loving tone.

"I, I . . . can't do this," Martha managed to spit out between choked up breaths muffled by tearful sniffles.

"Sure you can, Martha. Do you think I would have allowed you to stay in my school if I didn't believe you could do it? Martha, you have a feel for dance I've never seen before. You have a gift to share with the world! But, dear, if you allow the opinions of others to dictate your decisions for you, the world will never know your gift. The world needs to know, Martha. The world needs to know."

Martha was unsure. What would people think of her? What would her friends think of her? Would she ever hear from her mom or dad again? And then there were her fellow dancers; they still looked at her like she was an outcast. So what was this gift Ruth saw in her?

Years went by as Martha continued to train at The Denishawn School. One evening, Ruth St. Denis came to see Martha perform.

Although she was very talented, Ruth could see the callousness that had built up within Martha; it was time to push her to go do what she was destined to do: change the way dance was viewed by the world.

"Martha, can we meet for coffee tomorrow?" Not thinking much of it, Martha agreed and the next morning cheerfully arrived at a quaint café.

"Yes, what did you want to discuss?" Martha asked as she skimmed the menu.

"I don't think you were made for this."

Martha's heart plummeted to her ankles, along with the menu she had been holding. Her posture crumbled. "All these years, and now you tell me I'm not made for this? You told me that you believed in me!" Martha thought as she sat in the chair frozen. "What do you mean?" Martha muttered while choking back tears.

"Martha, dear, you are made for more than anything the Denishawn school can give you. You have the ability to change the way dance is viewed forever! You are the *queen of modern dance*."

That phrase echoed in Martha's mind, *the queen of modern dance*. What did she mean? How could she, an average-looking outcast by nature, change the way dance is viewed forever?

"So where am I supposed to go?" Martha asked, hoping Ruth was just playing a practical joke on her.

"Move to New York. You will find it. It won't be easy, but trust me you will find it."

Later that evening as Martha was packing her bags, a lump boiled up in her throat, and finally she burst into tears. Should she go through with this? What if Ruth was wrong? What if the people in New York wouldn't accept her? What if NO ONE would ever accept her? All Martha wanted to do was fit in. All she wanted was the approval of her mother, her friends, and her peers. Why did she have to long for more?

The Crux

Does Martha take action by going on to New York and changing the way dance is viewed forever, introducing modern dance to the world? Or does she pack her bags, go home, and live a life of fitting in?

***

Ten seconds. That's it. Ten quick seconds is the average amount of time that another person spends thinking about you when they pass you on the street.

Meanwhile, you feel judged, beaten down, debilitated, incapable of taking your next step. Those minuscule ten seconds crush you. You allow them to invade your very being and hijack the next 86,390 of your seconds. The quick comment, facial expression, or even just assumed opinion of another person who spent approximately ten seconds thinking about you now consumes your thoughts and has multiplied into 86,390 seconds. And guess what? There are only 86,400 seconds in a day, so you do the math.

When the opportunity to take action arises, why would you take it if you know the approval rating won't be there? It's hard to step out of the norm and stand out from the crowd, because *different* isn't always the most welcomed. It's much easier to jump on the bandwagon than it is to start your own.

I understand. From a young age most of us are conditioned to "fit in." To find a group of friends who think like you, act like you, and share your same values. You strove to fit the mold with childhood friends, and continue to do it now in your close social circle, around peers at work, on social media, and so on. More than anything, you want to *fit in*. But life is not "one size fits all."

So why are you so concerned about what others think of you? Picture this: you're in the middle of the game, playing the best you have all season, but the one bad shot you missed incites a fan sitting behind the bench to jeer at you every time you touch the ball. You can't shake his disapproval; it infects your mind and pretty soon, it feels like everyone is rooting against you. A side glance from your coach, a quick comment from your teammate, slowly it all takes over and leads you to play the remainder of the game extremely safe in hopes that you won't further upset anyone else. Why risk putting yourself in the light of scrutiny again? The game ends, and your team loses by a few points— points you know you could have scored had you had the courage to be bold.

So why does the opinion of someone else, someone who doesn't have to personally live with the weight of your daily decisions or ever step foot in your shoes, become capable of determining whether or not you take action? Ask yourself that question out loud. And then again. No matter how many times you do, it makes zero sense. Allowing yourself to fall victim to other people's opinions and be paralyzed by them isn't actually logical.

Welcome to the greatest prison: fearing what other people think, Camp *Allodoxaphobia*.

The Brain

Neuroscience supports that your current fear of other people's opinions is a conditioned response that began in childhood. Did you show up to school with a toy that other kids didn't deem popular? In middle school, did you bring ethnic food your mom packed for you that the other kids called smelly or funny? In high school, did you have to drive your parents' beaten-down station wagon? In college, did a teacher scoff at you in front of the entire class when you suggested an alternative theory to something? Add all of those experiences, and more just like it, to the database of future triggers for *allodoxaphobia*.

Allodoxaphobia is the irrational fear of hearing other people's opinions, being ridiculed by other people, someone stronger not agreeing with you, or looking like a fool. The word *allodoxaphobia* comes from Greek *allom* meaning different, *dox*, meaning opinion, and *phobos*, which comes from the Greek god of fear.

Fast-forward to adulthood. A new coworker is being excluded from a happy hour invite after work. You really like this coworker, but after years of striving, you are finally considered a member of the "in crowd" and you dare not risk your status. This new coworker is smart and could help you be more productive, come up with innovative ideas, and further your mission. But those triggers from childhood, middle school, high school, college, and so on have grown and grown and grown over time. They've matured into a mental fearmonger, one that will do anything it can to keep you at the status quo. So instead of taking action and befriending this new coworker, you just follow along with the others. Correction: you are taking action by doing this; it just isn't the type of action you need.

One of the main players in why you fear other people's opinions is the medial prefrontal cortex (mPFC), a part of the "social brain." (The diagram can be found online at www.davidnurse.com.)

mPFC has been shown to play a fundamental role in a wide range of social cognitive abilities such as self-reflection, person perception, and Theory of Mind/mentalizing. It serves as a key region in understanding self and others, and is viewed as the domain active in learning and predicting the likely outcomes of actions. For a long time, scientists believed this part of the brain didn't develop until a person went through puberty. However, neuroimaging studies with infants provide evidence that mPFC exhibits functional activation much earlier, suggesting that the mPFC is involved in social information processing from very early on in life.

According to another study done by scientists at the Max Planck Institute for Human Cognitive and Brain Sciences (MPI CBS), University College London, and the Social Neuroscience Lab Berlin, it has been discovered that children as young as age four can already determine what others think about them.

Children are able to perceive and interpret the mental states of people in their environment. Because a child's reasoning abilities are still developing, however, their perceived event becomes their reality. This phenomenon is called Theory of Mind (ToM), which refers to the capacity to understand other people by assuming the mental states they are in (i.e., predicting and suspecting what state of mind the other person is in. This is commonplace, a subconscious practice we all participate in when we meet someone: initially judging, analyzing, and inferring others' state of mind). Children use it to explain and predict another person's actions. Theory of Mind can be explicit or implicit. Explicit, meaning there is no room left for confusion or doubt. Every detail is cut and dry, black and white. Implicit, meaning implied, open for interpretation, not clearly expressed.

Explicitly, children interpret physical actions or words for what they are taught the actions and words mean. Implicitly, children interpret the unsaid messages from adults, including body language or tone of voice. Implicit messages have shown to be more powerful in influencing children's behavior than explicit messages. For example, say a parent rolls his eyes at a child when the child is having a meltdown. Regardless of the parent's intention, the child interprets this action to mean that his or her feelings are unacceptable. The child may begin hiding his or her feelings from the parent. The way you interpreted events as a child can affect whether or not you take action today.

A specific area of the brain that is active early on in childhood is the supramarginal gyrus. The supramarginal gyrus plays a huge role in a person's ability to process written, verbal, and emotional responses. It interprets, or in most cases imagines, others' nonverbal cues, especially those prompted by what we say and do. Eighty percent of communication is nonverbal. So a quick smirk, a confused look, or a negative darting glance from somebody in reaction to something you said or did in the past teaches your brain to expect that same response in the future. Your brain now associates this isolated outcome with all future outcomes, conditioning your brain to both expect and fear looking foolish again.

The temporoparietal junction is associated with auditory and somatosensory feelings and is also active by age four. If you heard a parent use an unaffectionate tone during childhood, you will quickly associate that tone with a negative feeling even into adulthood.

When you base your actions on the opinion of others throughout your life, at the core you are seeking validation. The area of the brain associated with validation-seeking is known as the *ventral striatum*. It is an area of the brain that sits in the center, just above and behind your ears and is considered to be the reward center. Studies have shown that if someone whom we consider to be an "expert" validates our actions, the ventral striatum lights up, cueing a rush of dopamine and a rewarding feeling in our brain. The more validation we get, the more the ventral striatum lights up.

Validation becomes the driving force behind the decisions we make and the action we take. It enables you to feel safe in moving forward.

- Your spouse tells you they really like the way your body looks in that dress, so that dress is now a wardrobe staple.

- You receive a flood of praise for the pitch idea you presented, so the confidence you have in your creative abilities heightens.

Remember when we mentioned heuristics at the beginning of the book—the shortcuts our brain creates to make snap decisions? Well, here is why they are so important in our brain's decision-making process. Heuristics take all the learned cognitive responses associated with what others think of us and create shortcuts.

The three types are availability, representative, and affect.

- *Availability heuristics* is based on recall of recent exposure to a situation. If your coworker spoke up in a board meeting and was immediately shot down, or you binged a TV show where the main character was ridiculed because he tried to stand out, your mental shortcut will remind you immediately to avoid any situation that could result in a similar outcome.

- *Representative heuristics* is the association of someone in our current life with someone from our past. If your boss resembles your fifth-grade teacher—the teacher who laughed out loud when you volunteered for the spelling bee after you failed your last spelling assignment—your confidence will likely falter when you are around your boss.

- *Affect heuristics* is purely based on how you are feeling in the current moment. If your most recent post on social media where you shared a vulnerable moment just got the lowest amount of likes you have ever received, then your likelihood to open up to friends and loved ones will lessen.

So, now we know how and why the brain reacts to fear of other people's opinions in the way it does. But how does the feeling in our heart hold us back?

The Heart

In 1902, Charles Horton Cooley put forth the looking-glass self theory to describe the process of people basing their sense of self-worth and value on what they perceive *others* believe of them.

Social interaction is the mirror, and the reflection we see is the picture painted from someone else's viewpoint. Our heart, our self-belief, is shattered if the reflection seen is an un-affirming one.

Your heart cares about your feelings. And let me tell you it is damn hard to take action if you are focused on protecting your heart, fearful of feeling pain triggered by other people's opinions.

Your heart is the gatekeeper of your *allodoxaphobia*. No pain, no gain couldn't be more true. When you are overly concerned with other people's opinions, you will never allow your heart to feel the pain it actually needs to grow.

Rest assured, "God is faithful, and he will not let you be tested beyond your strength but with your testing he will also provide the way out so that you may be able to endure it" (1 Corinthians 10:13).

There is no denying that, at some level, you strive for the approval of others. You feel the sting of rebuke more powerfully than you do the joy of praise. Seeking approval has caused you to care so much about what others think about you, that in turn you stop being *you*.

Think about how much better your world would be if you didn't concern yourself with what everyone around you thinks about you.

Will they laugh at me if I speak up?

Will my idea be shot down and called stupid?

Will my teammates still talk to me if they find out I'm a Christian?

What if my parents don't approve of the career path I love?

What if the new person I'm dating realizes I don't drink and thinks I'm weird?

What if this picture I post on social media doesn't get any likes?

The handcuffs of fear cut to the bone, and unless we give our brains and our hearts the permission to let go of the thoughts flowing through the minds of others, we will never become the person we were made to be.

In what is widely considered to be the greatest landslide vote in the history of US presidential elections, Richard Nixon defeated George McGovern in 1972 with 60.7% of the popular vote. This is considered a massive landslide victory. Do you know what that means? That means 39.3.% of the American population disliked Nixon.

Not everyone is going to like you, and that's just the honest truth you are going to have to come to terms with. You want approval, you enjoy approval, you seek approval, but you don't *need* approval. You *need* your heart to beat to survive. You don't *need* approval to survive. This innate desire for approval is what causes our paralysis from taking action and in turn leads to a life of passivity.

But remember, passive action is still action. You are consciously making the decision to play it safe and live a life dictated by fear. But here's the good news: with increased awareness and the right tools, which I will show you, you can rewire your brain to overcome its conditioning, stop guarding your heart, and take the action you have desperately longed for.

WHAT ACTUALLY HAPPENED TO MARTHA?

As Martha boarded the train set for New York on that crisp fall morning in 1925 she wondered if her life would ever be the same. Is she making the right decision? Will she regret leaving the Denishawn school? Are her mother and close friends right? Are her dreams senseless? Should she be focused on caring for a home and family instead of pursuing something as impossible as completely changing the world of dance?

After the long train ride, Martha headed directly to the Eastman School of Music in Rochester, New York. She spent the next year not only performing but also teaching. The confidence she gained showed her she really did have a gift to share with the world. She began to choreograph her own dances. Slowly, she began to shed the weight of other's opinions; she was no longer afraid to stand out. Martha's creativity began to explode. On a mission, Martha moved to New York City and into a tiny Carnegie Hall studio. She founded her own school in 1926: the Martha Graham Center for Contemporary Dance.

Martha's expression of dance told meaningful stories, shed light on important current events, and brought strong emotions to a stage where strong emotions were once frowned on. People didn't take well to the style at first. It was worlds apart from the European ballet they were familiar with. But Martha learned not to care; she kept on going. And as time passed, her exciting, novel form of expression grew in popularity.

People began to flock to New York City to watch the stories Martha's choreographed dances told. Martha was the first dancer to perform at the White House. She was invited by President Franklin Roosevelt and even taught the first lady, Eleanor Roosevelt, how to dance. Martha would go on to perform for seven more presidents. She was the first dancer to ever receive America's highest civilian award, the Medal of Freedom, and was the first to tour abroad as a cultural ambassador,

Martha choreographed and danced for over 70 years, creating 181 unique works. The impact she had on the art of dance has put her in the same category as other revolutionary artists such as Pablo Picasso or Frank Lloyd Wright. She became known as "Dancer of the Century."

The world of dance, and the world itself, was changed forever.

The same Martha Graham who had once lived in paralyzing fear of other people's opinions, who was told she was too average and her dreams would amount to nothing, changed the world just as she sought out to do.

She took action when it wasn't easy. She took action when it wasn't the popular decision. She took action when the people closest to her judged her.

Go to any Broadway show today, watch any dance movie, or maybe even go to the local pub and watch people dancing after they have had one too many, and you will see the impact Martha Graham had on the world.

FLIP THE SCRIPT

Here is a hypothetical look at your life if Martha Graham had never taken action. If she'd let the fear of other people's opinions uproot her dream to change the world through dance. If she hadn't broken the mold of ballet and been the crucial segue for all future choreographers and technique innovators to follow suit.

- You're in New York City on a business trip and thrilled to have two tickets to the world-famous Broadway play *Hamilton*. But instead of watching a play with so much creativity, rhythm, and cultural style, you watch Lin-Manuel Miranda dance around the stage performing in pointe shoes executing ássembles and arabesques.

- You return to your home in the suburbs. It's Tuesday afternoon, time to get your daughters to their dance class at the local dance studio. Your daughters are preparing for a hip-hop concert later that month—the state championships. But much to your surprise, instead of bouncing to the up-tempo beats, your daughters look more like they're practicing for Tchaikovsky's *Swan Lake*.

- You've got a four-day weekend ahead of you, and you've agreed to spend it at your in-laws'. You've been there for two days already and need to clear your head and maybe grab a drink.

You head down to the local pub, and see it's a country-themed bar. A surefire sign they'll have line dancing, your favorite. As you walk into the garish bar, you're met with the crooning twang of country music. *Ahh*, all is right in the world again, until, that is, you look at the dance floor and discover it's not line dancing you see; it's not even the waltz, the polka ten-step, or the traveling cha-cha. Instead, in the center of the rowdy honky-tonk, you find the world's most ethereal form of dance, European ballet.

"What has happened to the world?" You think aloud in each of these scenarios.

And then you realize, Martha never took action. She decided not to go to New York and open her own dance studio. She never revolutionized the dance world with an entirely new style. Instead, she went back to her hometown, like her mother and friends had told her she should do, and lived out the remainder of her years as a housewife. Modern dance was never born. Dance and theater were never revolutionized. Sadly, Martha had given into the fear of other people's opinions, and it held her back from realizing her destiny.

Remember, there are 86,400 seconds in a day. How many of those seconds are you going to waste allowing the opinions of others to control the decisions you make today?

No one else puts on your shoes every day; you do. You are the expert in you, not your friend who only sees a snapshot of your life. You are the decision-maker of your destiny, not your mother who wants your life to be as easy and safe as possible. You have a decision to make, right here, right now. You can either let Allodoxaphobia be your north star, or you can say "Other people can have their opinions, and opinions can have other people." But not you.

You take action.

TOOLS TO OVERCOME THE ALLODOXAPHOBIC

You've felt it before, and it was oh-so-liberating. That judgmental comment torpedoed toward you and the pain was supposed to ensue, but then . . . it didn't come. There was no feeling behind the words meant to slay your day. You didn't flinch, you didn't care. But why? And how?

You laughed at yourself.

Wait, what? Aren't you trying to act like you have it all together and *avoid* any laughter?

Quite the opposite actually.

It all depends on the context of *how* we laugh at ourselves. According to psychologist and humor researcher Arnie Cann, it's *how* we choose to use humor that leads to a positive or negative response. Laughter has been scientifically proven to release dopamine, increase blood flow, and strengthen the heart. Even more so, it enables us to boost our resiliency with increased optimism.

But it all comes down to the way we laugh at ourselves, the type of self-jab we take. If we throw a hay-making uppercut that we're not ready for, it will knock us out cold. But if we take a small jab to our own gut, the laughter will not only free us from caring about the opinions of others, but will also give others permission to do the same in their lives.

Take risks, dance in public, profess your love for your spouse so the whole world can hear, embrace your quirky side. Permission to be true to who you are has fully been granted.

The world needed Martha to be who she truly was. And the world needs you to be who you truly are.

The tools: In the "Tools" section throughout the book, you'll learn actionable tools to overcome roadblocks the brain and heart emit and turn the knowledgeable *whys* into actionable *hows*. You will also learn how to implement to tools in order to take action today! (Examples of all the tools throughout this book can be found online at www.davidnurse.com.)

Learn to Be a Comedian

To overcome fear of other people's opinion, you need to learn to be a comedian. How are you going to make yourself laugh today? First let's start with this: What is your comedy name? For example, Cedric the Entertainer? Larry the Cable Guy?

Create a name for yourself that gives you the permission to be funny. All the great comedians poke fun at themselves; they know how to throw the correct self-jab that will open up the audience so they can feel better about themselves.

Action step for the day: Figure out your comedic stage name and find some way to laugh at yourself today.

For example, I've named myself Dancing David. Today when I see someone in public who is stressed, I'm going to ask them what their favorite song is. When they tell me their favorite song, I'm going to play it out loud on my phone and start dancing. It is a risk, but laughing at myself and my terrible dance moves will help me shed the fear of others' opinions and hopefully alleviate some stress in their life.

Put this into action. You can first test this out on a family member. Afterwards, make the commitment to putting this action into motion the next time you go out in public, to a grocery store, coffee shop, or wherever it may be. Commit to yourself this won't only be a one-and-done action. The more you do it, the more the positive benefit will occur for both you and others.

Create a Personal Mantra

Companies have mission statements hanging on their office walls, sports teams have culture declarations plastered all over the locker room, and you need to have your own *personal mantra* in your pocket at all times.

Your personal mantra is a funnel of clarity for who you are so *you* control the narrative of your life, not others' opinions. A personal mantra encompasses what you stand for and expresses who you say you are to the world.

Our internal narrative is like a radio station, and the station will continue to play until you turn the dial. You control what is called your *narrative psychology.*

Waterloo University professors Ian McGregor and John Holmes found that if you provide people with an ambiguous story about a breakup and then ask them to tell a slanted story that places the blame on just one of the parties involved, the people begin to believe their own story. This shows the stories (mantras) we tell ourselves carry immense power in shaping our memory of an event.

Once you tell yourself a story, it's hard to get out of that story's framework. The question becomes, what story are *you* telling yourself?

The word *mantra* literally means "a statement or slogan repeated frequently."

Action step for the day: Come up with your own personal mantra. To start, ask yourself these three questions:

- What are my strongest qualities?

- What are my favorite words?

- What type of people do I enjoy being around?

Once you have answered these questions, you can begin to shape your *own* personal mantra. Here is an example:

- My strongest qualities are encouragement and energy.

- My favorite words are *bravery*, *exuberant*, and *ambience*.

- I enjoy being around people who make me feel like I can be 100% myself and there is no judgment.

So, my personal mantra becomes this: *I create an environment of exuberant encouragement.*

With every room I enter, I want to be able to walk into the room with this mantra plastered on my brain. It will help shape the way I view myself and the way I interact with and treat others.

Where do you keep your personal mantra? Somewhere you can see it every day multiple times per day! I have mine written on the lock screen of my phone (I highly advise you do the same). Every time I touch my phone (which is more than I'd like to admit), it will be a subconscious reminder to live out my mantra. I also have mine written down on a small piece of paper, placed in my wallet. This is a reminder of how much my personal mantra is worth. Bonus point if you put your personal mantra on your lock screen and in your wallet!

YOUR ACTION ANIMAL: THE HIPPO

Whose skin are you wearing? What if you went into every conversation with this mentality: "How can I become so comfortable in my own skin that I'm able to make the others in the room comfortable in theirs, too?"

Do you think that would take a weight off your shoulders as you stepped through the doors? How freeing would it be to no longer worry about what others thought of you, but instead how you could make them feel?

One way to overcome the fear of other people's opinions is to grow hippopotamus skin. Yes, I did just say hippo skin. The hippopotamus secretes orange and red pigment molecules out of their skin's pores, creating the illusion they are sweating out blood. These compounds are acidic and help to protect against infection. The red pigment is hipposudoric acid and the orange is norhipposudoric acid, both amino acid metabolites.

Source: nilsversemann/Adobe Stock

The hippo has some of the roughest, unsmooth skin in all the animal kingdom. Essentially, they are *calloused*, just like human beings become if they build up armor-thick skin that defends against the sword of other people's opinions. But instead of staying hardened and apathetic, the hippo releases the red and orange acid to lubricate and protect their skin, essentially softening their hardened outer shell.

Once you lay down your guard and soften your skin instead of curling up in your shell of personal protection, you will allow yourself to become impenetrable to the opinions of others.

Be the hippo! No matter what your skin looks like or feels like, be comfortable in your own skin. And by doing so, you allow other "hiding hippos" around you to secrete their colorful amino acid metabolites.

"What people in the world think of you is really none of your business."

—Martha Graham

CHAPTER 2

The Burned

MEET LEWIS LATIMER

"How old are you, boy?" the Navy admiral aggressively asked young Lewis Latimer, while in line waiting to enroll for the Civil War.

"Eighteen years old, sir," Lewis replied.

The truth was, Lewis was only 16. He was lying about his age so he could enroll in the Navy to help provide for his mother and siblings. He was the youngest of four children born to George and Rebecca Latimer, both of whom had escaped enslavement and fled to the North.

Lewis's father, who had once been a superhero to Lewis, was no longer around to provide for the family. He walked out years earlier when his family needed him the most. Even though no one knew of his exact whereabouts, Lewis was told his father ran away to escape being sent back to the South following the *Dred Scott* decision in 1857. But young Lewis couldn't decipher the difference; all he knew was that his father abandoned him.

Lewis's siblings pushed Lewis forward, against his will, pouring their hope into him. Lewis had a fatal flaw that would continue to rear its head and bite him: gullible *trust*. Throughout his childhood, Lewis always saw the best in people, wanting to believe he could depend on them. But every time he allowed himself to trust, he got burned. And the burns by his family left the deepest scars.

"Okay, boy, get on the ship. And I don't want a word out of you," ordered the admiral. Lewis nodded his head and shuffled onto the ship where he would spend the next year at sea. "Why does everyone leave me?" Lewis would often wonder while lying on the deck underneath the stars. Lewis would find himself in this position often, back on the deck, eyes to the sky, cursing God, and demanding a divine "break."

One day during a battle, Lewis was badly injured. While lying in his hospital bed, he cried out, "Why can't I just catch a break; nothing I do ever works out. What's the point of continuing on?"

While in recovery, Lewis's hospital roommate entertained him with stories about the wonderful things he learned in school. Things like science, math, and mechanical drawings. With no formal access to education, Lewis was forced to learn everything on his own. Inspired, Lewis spent his remaining days of recovery teaching himself how to master the craft of mechanical drawing. "Maybe this will make the Navy want to keep me long term!" he thought excitedly.

But at the end of the war, Lewis was relieved of his Naval duties. He received an honorable discharge and was dumped off at the port of Boston with nothing but wound scars and haunting memories of battle.

"Honorable discharge, *hmmpph*," Lewis muttered as he stepped off the ship in Boston. "Ain't nothing honorable about taking a bullet in the leg. Now how am I going to get employment? No one wants a Black, wounded soldier without a lick of formal schooling."

Lewis had trusted, and he was burned. Time after time. He trusted his father: gone. He trusted his family: they sold him out to the Navy. He trusted the Navy: they tossed him aside.

Burned by the past time and time again. On his way to becoming bittered by the past.

Lewis spent day after day wandering through the streets of Boston, sleeping on street corners, looking for any type of work he could get. Uneducated, injured, without a dollar to his name, and living in an 1868 white man's world, Lewis faced what seemed like an insurmountable challenge. Then, one day, as Lewis ambled past the law firm of Crosby and Gould, a flyer caught his eye that read "OFFICE BOY NEEDED."

"How hard can that be?" Lewis thought. "I don't need any educational training; it's not manual labor. I'm sure I can figure this out." Lewis walked into the law firm, trying his best not to draw attention to his dirty clothes and what he assumed was a pungent personal aroma.

"May I help you?" The assistant asked from behind the front desk.

"Yes, ma'am, I'm here for the office boy job," Lewis stated with clear conviction.

"Take a seat, son, and someone will be right with you," she replied.

Could he actually get this job? Or was he just getting his hopes up only to be burned again?

"Mr. Gould will see you now," the assistant announced.

Knees shaking, Lewis made his way down the narrow hallway toward Mr. Gould's office.

"The job is yours if you want it," Mr. Gould announced, taking Lewis by surprise.

With a spring in his step, Lewis left the office feeling a little taller. Monday morning, he clocked in as the new office boy for Crosby and Gould Law Firm.

Lewis worked hard for years and went on to have success at the firm; what he had taught himself about mechanical drawing in the Navy made all the difference. His ability to sketch patent drawings and creative visions for new products earned him a raise from $3 per week to $5 and eventually landed him the role of head draftsman, earning a whopping $20 per week.

He'd made it! He was going to be able to take care of his mother and siblings; he even met the affable Mary Wilson, the woman of his dreams. The past that had once burned him was just that, a thing of the past. Lewis was finally living the good life.

That is, until one chilly winter day a few years later when Lewis's beloved boss and mentor, Mr. Gould, passed away. The new partner, Mr. Gregory, would take over the reins effective immediately.

"Fired?!" Lewis hollered. A devastating triple whammy of anger, shock, and betrayal hit him like a sucker punch straight to the gut. "How could this be?" he thought. "I'm the lead draftsman. I'm the best inventor they've got!"

Without a word of explanation, Lewis was asked to clear his desk and vacate the office by day's end.

Determined to know the reason for his abrupt termination, Lewis stormed into Mr. Gregory's office. "What is happening here, Mr. Gregory?" Lewis demanded.

After a deafening silence, Mr. Gregory looked him dead in the eyes. "Lewis, you are no longer needed here. Or wanted."

And that was it. Over. Once again, burned. Lewis's livelihood gone in the blink of an eye.

How could he go on? Where would he go? Was there anyone else who would give him work? And why even try if he was just going to get burned again? What would Mary think?

Months went by. Then, on a January morning in 1876, there was a knock at the Latimers' front door. "Who could be knocking this early in the morning?" Lewis thought. "Mary, are you expecting someone?" he asked his wife.

"No, dear, I'm not. But don't just sit there; go answer the door and see who it is," she replied with a hint of hope in her voice.

"Hello, is this the residence of Mr. Latimer?" the stocky Scottish man in the top hat asked from the front doorstep.

"Yes, I am he," Lewis replied in a monotone voice.

"I'm wondering if you can help me with a project. I heard you are the best patent draftsman in the land. I'm working on an invention that I think can change the world. But I can't do it alone. I need your help," the man revealed with zeal.

Thoughts scattered through Lewis's mind. Who was this random stranger? How did he hear about me? Why does he need my help? If

I agree to this, will I just end up getting let down again, like everyone has done to me in the past?

"What did you say your name was again, sir?" Lewis asked.

"Alexander Graham Bell," the man replied.

THE CRUX

Does Lewis agree to help Alexander Graham Bell and potentially change the world? Or does he turn the offer down in fear of being burned again?

***

You trusted them. You gave them everything you had. And like a massive Everest avalanche, it all came crashing down without a single snowflake of a warning.

Burned.

Why ever trust again if your heart is just going to be torn out of your chest? We've all been there, and it hurts.

There is no easy way around it; getting burned leaves a scar. A wound so deep, you think the mangled tissue will never repair. But the scar itself isn't a mark of *loss*; it's actually the entry way for the light of your purpose to filter through.

I get it; it's much easier to nurse your wound than it is to put yourself out there again and again. You loved her but she betrayed you. How could you ever love again? You trusted your business partner, but he stole from you. How could you ever go into business again? You put years into the start-up, only to see it go bankrupt. Why even try to build another business? Logic tells us that if we get burned once, it will happen again.

And maybe it will. But I can tell you this: if you think you'll be able to avoid hardship, pain, and failure and strike success the first time you try something, you are kidding yourself. Being burned is a part of the process.

Walt Disney was fired by the *Kansas City Star* newspaper because he wasn't *creative* enough. Jerry Seinfeld was jeered at and booed off stage in his first stand-up comedy performance. Elvis Presley's manager told him to go back to driving a truck after his first concert. Colonel Sanders's fried chicken recipe was rejected 1,009 times before it was finally accepted. R. H. Macy, one of the most successful American businessmen of all time, had four stores fail and go bankrupt before he hit it big with Macy's Department Store. The list goes on and on.

Understand that you *will* get burned. The choice you make is whether to let that burn become a defining scar or an enlightening scar.

A closer look at how the brain and heart processes painful past events will help you better understand that you have a choice in the type of scar you choose to wear. A scar that paralyzes future action or a scar that shapes your purpose.

The Brain

Being burned by the past is a form of trauma. When you experience a traumatic event, adrenaline rushes through the body engulfing the amygdala. The amygdala then holds the emotional significance of the event, acting as an internal compass, advising you to avoid any future similar scenarios.

This is why it is so difficult to put yourself out there after being burned. You are now living in the "what-if" mode.

Think about it like this: your brain is a picture reel of memories. Each picture is stored in the prefrontal cortex, where the rational decision-making area of the brain occurs. If the trauma trigger is ignited, our prefrontal cortex gives us three decisions to make: fight, flight, or freeze. Although these actions support survival, none of the three choices are ideal for long-term growth.

The only way to overcome past trauma is to desensitize the emotional response to the trigger (which we will get into more later on in this chapter).

Understanding the way your brain processes past pain will enable you to make sense of your what-ifs and the power you're giving them to paralyze you from taking action.

What if you quit your job to go all in on your passion, but you can't make a buck? What if you finally decide to step on stage to speak and you can't remember the words? What if you ask your dream girl out on a date and she turns you down in front of your friends? What if you . . . (fill in the blank).

The root in the what-ifs is fear.

But the question I'm here to propose should grip you with even more fear: "What if you don't?" What if you don't take the chance going all in on your passion? You will live in eternal regret. What if you don't take the chance to step on stage to speak? You will live with the guilt of knowing you could have made a bigger impact. What if you don't ask your dream girl out on a date? You might miss out on finding Ms. Right.

The past isn't just capable of *burning* you; it can also *freeze* you.

According to trauma specialist Carla Marie Manly, PhD, "When an individual is traumatized, especially early on in life, the memory of the trauma is stored in both the brain and the body."

If healing doesn't occur, the brain and body can hold onto this trauma, affecting human development. Our past wounds have the ability to leave us frozen in the moment the trauma occurred. Meaning, even though you are in the current year physically, your body and mind can be stuck in the past.

Ask yourself if you suffer from any of the following:

- Fear-based behaviors, such as excessive anxiety or controlling behavior
- A tendency to shut down or dissociate
- People-pleasing behavior
- Knowing you want to do something in life, but feel like you can't get there

- Easily feeling emotionally overwhelmed

- Unstable interpersonal relationships and difficulty maintaining healthy relationships

These are signals you are still holding on to a traumatic moment from the past that has frozen you in that time. This is known as *trauma-associated age regression*. Some estimates state that at least 70% of adults in the US have experienced some sort of extreme trauma in their life. Trauma expert James S. Gordon states: "Everything that happens to us emotionally or psychologically happens to our bodies as well. It is all connected," he says. "If you look at people who go into a fight, flight, or freeze response, just look at the way they hold their bodies—they're tense, they're tight, their whole body is set up to protect them from a predator."

Take, for example, post-traumatic stress disorder (PTSD). It creates intense disruption in hormone secretion, neurochemical production, and immune system function—three components vital to our bodies' physical and mental health. Now we all think of PTSD being associated with soldiers coming home from war, but according to studies, up to 35% of chronic pain patients actually have PTSD.

So what does this all mean? Our brains *and* our bodies hold the traumas of our past. To overcome the action-taking roadblocks created by previous burns, it's crucial to release the traumas of our past.

The Heart

Our hearts are primed to imagine how life's past events could have turned out differently. When these thought processes run contrary to what actually happened (counter to the facts), we engage in counterfactual thinking. When considering the what-ifs of life, there are two types of people: those with *upward counterfactual thinking* and those with *downward counterfactual thinking*.

Upward counterfactual thinking is when you look back on a situation and imagine how it could have been better; it's always second-guessing your past choices. This type of thinking makes you believe that if you would have made different choices, your life right now would be improved.

> "What if I wouldn't have told my significant other who I truly am?" She wouldn't have ended the relationship.

> "What if I wouldn't have put so much time into helping my boss after they said they would give me a raise?" I could have had time to start my own business.

> "What if I wouldn't have gone into the business deal with my family member?" My life would be so much freer now.

As we already know, the what-ifs can be killers. But, when looked at with a fresh perspective, they can also be life-givers.

Downward counterfactual thinking is when you look back on the what-ifs of a situation and you can see how things could have actually been worse; therefore, you're confident you made the right choices. You believe if you had made different choices, then your life would not be as good as it is right now.

It's the most powerful perspective shift there is.

I'm so glad I went to the dinner with all of those people who make more money than I do, who have more followers than I do, and who are more recognized publicly than I am. What if I would have said no? I wouldn't have those people in my network, and I feel like I belong at those tables now!

I'm thankful I pursued my dreams of starting my own company, even though it flopped the first two times and it took years to get off the ground. What if I hadn't gone for it? I can't imagine not having the experience of how to grow a business and the autonomy I have now.

Which type of thinking is most common for you?

It's like the aftermath of a forest fire—do you see the forest charred in ruins or do you see the forest ripe to birth new life? Your perspective contributes to what I call bounce-back-ability—the ability to hit the ground and bounce, not splatter. We have all been fired or rejected. I have, you have. It's not the end—as long as you live in downward counterfactual thinking and practice bounce-back-ability.

Take, for example, my favorite tree, the palm tree. Even when the strongest of storms brutally beat down on it, the palm tree bends but never breaks. Even when hurricane speed winds test the depths of its roots, it doesn't budge, it grows even deeper roots.

Life gives you two choices for dealing with failure: you can either let the failure in your past keep you from reaching your future success or you *learn* from past failures to lead you to your greatest success.

Lewis Latimer's future boss Thomas Edison said it best: "People give up because they don't know how close they are to success."

What if I told you that you are one more failure away from your greatest success? One more "getting burned" away from reaching your destiny? One more *what-if* moment away from becoming the person you were made to be? Would you keep going, or would you give up?

WHAT ACTUALLY HAPPENED TO LEWIS LATIMER?

Lewis stood on his doorstep face to face with Alexander Graham Bell. Lewis could just say no, thank you, send Alexander on his way, and go back inside to nurse his old wounds. Just as he was about to turn down the job, he glanced over at his wife and suddenly the perspective of his past what-ifs shifted—what if his father and mother had never escaped slavery, what if he hadn't been relieved of his duties from the Navy, what if he had never followed his gut about the Crosby and Gould flyer, what if he had never met his beautiful wife, what if, what if, what if? The positives of his past suddenly outshined the wounds.

Now he had to ask himself another what-if: What if he doesn't accept this job? He might be one yes away from his destiny. With new determination, Lewis accepted the job offer from Alexander Graham

Bell to assist in inventing and illustrating the patent for a small project called *the telephone.*

Upon accepting the job, the multimillion-dollar race was on and the duo had stiff competition. Elisha Gray, an American engineer, and Antonio Meucci, an Italian engineer, were independently working to complete patents for similar inventions. Lewis worked tirelessly to help Bell complete the invention and patent application first. On February 14, 1876, Lewis turned in the application just hours before Gray or Meucci attempted to turn in theirs. The patent office didn't require a working model to secure the rights. All they required was the thorough patent description, drawing, and application—and luckily for Bell, Lewis excelled at all three.

Because of Lewis Latimer's tenacity and skill, Alexander Graham Bell is enshrined in history books forever as the inventor of the telephone.

But Lewis didn't bask in the well-earned glory and stop taking action there. He was just getting started. In 1879, he accepted the job as the manager and drafter for the U.S. Electric Lighting Company in Bridgeport, Connecticut. The owner was a man named Hiram Maxim. Maxim was the chief rival to Thomas Edison, who had just recently invented incandescent light. But Edison's bulbs ran too hot and were extremely inefficient; they would glow but burn out shortly thereafter.

Maxim was convinced he could improve on Edison's invention and that Lewis would be the ace up his sleeve. Latimer instantly undertook the systematic study of electricity and its application to the problem of lighting, mastering its complexities in no time. He was able to increase the overall life span of the light bulb, the quality of the filament, and the arc lighting.

His resolve and action paid off. Thomas Edison was so impressed that he hired Lewis to come work directly for him. Lewis was appointed as the head of several different teams working in major cities such as Philadelphia, New York City, and Montreal to wire their roadways with electrical lighting. Lewis Latimer literally illuminated the United States.

He drafted patent sketches, searched for and reviewed patent infringement documents, and even testified in court on Edison's behalf. His prowess in the courtroom helped win Edison a crucial dispute over the invention of the carbon filament lamp; this win helped solidify Thomas Edison's name in history as the inventor of the light bulb. All thanks to Lewis Latimer.

The boy who grew up poor, without formal schooling or training, went on to author many books and pieces of work. Lewis wrote the first book on electric lighting in 1880, *Incandescent Electric Lighting*. He wrote poetry, prose, and plays for African American journals! Lewis was a Renaissance man who enjoyed painting and playing the flute.

This man—who had every excuse in the world to sit back and lick his wounds—did anything but wallow.

Latimer held strong to his faith in the country's fundamental promise of equality—and he didn't stand down to anyone. In 1903 Latimer bought a home in Flushing, New York (known for being a predominantly white community). His home became the meeting place for African American civic and cultural leaders.

Latimer used the platform he created through science and innovation to stand up for what he knew was right and what he knew was needed: *equality*.

Lewis spent the latter half of his life deeply involved in the community, founding several philanthropies, and became a backbone of leadership for the early Civil Rights movement.

Lewis Latimer was much more than an inventor; he took action to change the way the world treated mankind.

FLIP THE SCRIPT

Here's a hypothetical look at how different the world might be if Lewis hadn't taken action, if he had allowed his past hurts and fear of being burned again hold him back from accepting Alexander Graham Bell's offer.

You wake up before sunrise and roll over to reach for the lamp switch. But it's not there. There's no light. No electricity. The first incandescent light bulbs Thomas Edison created burned dangerously hot, causing so many fires throughout homes and communities that the National Patent Association had to prohibit the use of light bulbs.

Thankfully the sun will rise soon, filling your room with natural light. Then you'll get up, make your morning cup of joe, and start your day.

You sink into your pillow, close your eyes, and wait for the brightness of the outside world to greet your eyelids, signaling it's time to get up.

"Well, at least without my lamp I might get more sleep," you think to yourself as you climb the stairs.

You walk into the kitchen, heat the kettle, grind your coffee beans, and begin to slowly pour the steaming hot water over the redolence of the coffee grounds.

"All is right in the world again," you think as you breathe in the aroma.

You walk into the living room and sit down at your desk, taking in the beauty of the morning.

"What a great day ahead," you catch yourself saying out loud.

Today is your big phone call with the company you are going to acquire. If all goes right, you will own the company outright and set yourself up for incredible stock options once you take the company through its IPO.

The call is scheduled for 9 am. Good thing you got the extra hour of sleep, you are recharged and ready to dominate this call!

You reach into your pocket to grab your iPhone to start preparing for the call. Empty. You check your back pocket. Not there either. The coat you wore last night to dinner? Nope. The nightstand drawer where you often place your phone before bed? Negative again. Your heart starts to beat faster. You tell yourself not to panic. Well, that didn't last long; you are in full panic mode. How could this be? On the day of the biggest call of your life you can't find your phone?

You think on your feet, maybe your neighbor can call your phone and then you'll hear it vibrate. That's it, that'll work. Swiftly walking outside without even shutting the front door behind you, race over to your neighbor's house and knock vigorously on their door.

"Yes," your neighbor says as she opens the door, clearly confused by your early morning visit. "Is everything all right?"

"Can you please come over to my place and call my phone? I can't find it anywhere. I need it for a huge call I have in about 30 minutes, and I can't seem to remember where I put it. Would you be able to help? It'll only take a minute."

"Phone," she replies. "What is that?"

If Lewis Latimer had never taken action in that crucial moment when he accepted the job offer from Alexander Graham Bell, the two of them wouldn't have invented the phone together. You could argue that might be a good thing, but in the grand scheme of life, it's one of the greatest inventions ever created. Along with the incandescent light bulb, which wouldn't be what it is today without Lewis. He didn't allow being burned in his past deter him from his future—his future of changing the world.

TOOLS TO OVERCOME THE FEELING BURNED

Consider this scenario. You are in a very important company meeting, one that could make or break the entire organization. Your industry's landscape has shifted over the past few years, requiring a decision to either continue operations as usual or take a large risk with potential to ten times the company.

This is your area of expertise; you know the digital space inside and out.

Should you speak up and offer your insight and opinion? You did six months ago in the biannual meeting and immediately got shot down by your boss. The game is on the line and you've got the ball—are you going to take the shot?

Why risk putting yourself out there, in danger of a potential let-down by your boss and coworkers again? Is it actually worth it? So instead of speaking up, you remain silent, not wanting to repeat a previous outcome and relive the pain. As long as you don't say a word, no one can point a finger at you, and if no one can point a finger at you, then no one can blame you. And if no one can blame you, then you are safe from any line of fire. You're off the hook.

The company goes under four months later and files for bankruptcy. Deep down you know it was your fault. You let the past dictate your present and affect you and your entire company's future.

Here's the switch you need to flip: Instead of thinking "What if I miss" think "What if I *don't* take the shot?"

That is the mindset shift you need. You have prepared for this moment in your life, everything you have done has led up to your big moment, and if you turn it down because you are afraid of past events recurring, then you are essentially already digging your own grave and dying a slow death with your eyes wide open.

The past will always burn you, if you allow it to.

You know *why* you feel burned by the past; now it's time for me to show you how to conquer this archetype.

Nice to Meet You, "Little You": The Reverse Alter Ego

You have probably heard of Batman, Bruce Wayne's alter ego. Or The Black Mamba, Kobe Bryant's alter ego when he stepped on the court. Or maybe even Sasha Fierce, Beyonce's stage alter ego.

But what if I were to tell you the same concept used to create an alter ego can be used to detach the present you from the *you* of your past? Adopting an alter ego is a form of *self-distancing*. Rachel White, professor of psychology at Hamilton College, explains "self-distancing gives us a little bit of extra space to think rationally about the situation."

In a study done by Professor Ethan Kross at the University of Michigan, participants were asked to "think about a challenging event in the future, such as an important exam, in one of two different ways."

The groups were separated into two different conditions— *immersed* and *distanced*. The immersed group was told to look at the challenging event from the inside as if they were going through it. The distanced group was told to view the challenging event as if they were a fly on the wall, watching as an onlooker. The results were drastic, showing those with a distanced viewpoint felt much less anxiety about the event compared to the immersed group.

Why is this so important? If you view the *younger you* from the outside looking in, you're able to separate the person you were when you incurred past trauma from the person you are today.

The reverse alter ego enables you to free yourself of the burdens you have carried from your childhood.

> The kid who was verbally abused by their parents is no longer you.

> The high schooler who was made fun of at school is no longer you.

> The adult who was lied to by their business partner is no longer you.

> The spouse who was cheated on by their husband or wife is no longer you.

Today you have officially given yourself permission to distance yourself from the you who was burned. That is in your past; it does not define your present nor does it determine your future.

Action step for the day: Give yourself a reverse alter ego name. For example, mine is Little Davy. It makes me laugh when I say it out loud and reminds me that's who I was when I was younger, not today. I even use Little Davy for mistakes I made a few years ago, or when I think about the times I was burned in my life. Little Davy can have those past traumas, but not David. Not me. Not here, not now.

What is your reverse alter ego name? Decide what your name is going to be and begin to use it anytime you find yourself thinking negatively about past mistakes you have made.

And what past trauma do you need to reframe by using your new-born reverse alter ego? Try it now. Say out loud a past trauma that you have been unable to let go of. Use your reverse alter-ego name and allow yourself to realize that person in the past is not the person you are today. Bonus points for doing this exercise for all the past traumas you have!

Your AMS Pressure Points

When someone touches a bruise or a sore spot on your body, what happens? You flinch. You pull back. You might even mutter some obscenities in their direction. Your body is making the connection with your mind that you are hurting because of a physical trauma that occurred in your body. But what happens when that pressure point, instead of stemming from a physical blow, is mentally derived?

Studies have shown that when trauma occurs, the memory processing system in our brain can malfunction, shifting the trauma memory from the brain to the body without us even knowing. Talk about a sneak attack of all sneak attacks. Our brain, in attempt to process the trauma, reverts to encrypting pain and trauma into areas throughout our body.

According to Bradley Nelson, author of *The Emotion Code*, three things happen when an emotion is experienced:

- We develop an emotional vibration.

- We feel the emotion and any thoughts or physical sensations associated with it. This is where the mind and body's interconnectedness comes into play.

- We move on from the emotion by processing it.

This is the natural process our body and mind go through. However, when this process is interrupted in step two or three, the energy of the emotion becomes trapped in the body.

Ever wonder why it feels so good to get a massage and have the tension you are carrying in your shoulders released? Your body is releasing physical trauma, yes, but it's releasing the emotional trauma even more.

Can you overcome this? Can you find these pressure points on your body and release the trauma you have been storing up? Yes, and yes.

If you're like me, right now you are thinking, "Well, where in the body is my trauma being held?" A study done in 2013 led by a team of biomedical engineers in Finland sought to explain where emotions are felt in the body.

They mapped out the bodily reactions to emotions of 700 individuals, and what they found was fascinating. Different emotions were associated with different bodily sensations that were generally the same for all the participants. For example: anger, fear, and anxiety were held in the chest and upper body. To view the heat map Finnish engineers created to show where the trauma in the body is being held, go to www.davidnurse.com.

It's amazing to think the body can "keep score" of past traumas without you even knowing it, but it's more amazing to know the body can *heal itself*, making the human body the most incredible system on the planet.

Action Step for the Day: Acknowledgment, Movement, Stillness

For this tool, you'll use three actions to implement in your daily habits. There are options outlined after each point; you choose which one best suits your enjoyment and lifestyle. All it takes is five to ten minutes a day to go through this routine. Acknowledge the trauma and shake it out. Choose a form of movement you prefer. Finish with a couple minutes (or more) with complete stillness.

Acknowledgment

Label your feelings. Think of it as this: trauma is like elusive files and emails. No matter how hard you search for them, they are nowhere to be found. Now let's imagine you put those emails and files into a series of folders. These folders enable you to have control of the files and organizational peace because you know exactly where they are. The same thing happens with trauma. If you don't label it, then you are allowing it to be a shrapnel that continues to pierce your insides without you even being aware.

Acknowledge your trauma and place each traumatic experience in one of the following four folders:

- Fear—perceived threat, anxiousness
- Sadness—loss or rejection
- Disgust—unpleasant, unwanted situations
- Anger—injustice, wrongful unpunished acts

Now that you have labeled your trauma—acknowledged it—and know the areas in your body where it is held based on the heat map diagram, it's time to *shake it out*.

Movement

Movement has been proven to help the body deal with trauma. In fact, somatic experiencing (SE) movement is a type of movement that deals with trauma and is prescribed by a certified SE practitioner. It was developed by Dr. Peter Levine and helps the body release any painful, traumatic sensations it is holding on to. I recommend consulting a certified SE practitioner if you want to learn more. I'm not a doctor, but if you are looking for something you can do on your own, then let's move!

Choose your favorite form of these movements:

- Yoga
- Chi-gong
- Stretching
- Tai chi
- Martial arts

Or my favorite of these, just dance (whatever high-tempo dance movement you want)! I recommend beginning with at least five minutes a day.

Stillness

You have labeled your trauma and placed it in its folder; you have moved, increasing blood flow, which helps release the trauma. Now it's time to be still.

This quiet processing time is what scientists call *self-generation cognition*. By becoming still, you create the margins and space to allow emotions to come into consciousness. By disengaging from external stimuli, you connect with your thoughts, emotions, and desires.

This can look like any of the following:

- Mediation
- Breathing exercises
- Repeating affirmations
- Sitting in nature

Or my favorite: giving yourself permission to daydream!

YOUR ACTION ANIMAL: THE ECHIDNA

Let me introduce you to the spiny, Australian quill-covered anteater, the echidna, one of the only living mammals that lays eggs. But that's not the only thing that makes them unique, and that's not why I call them the "burned by the past" action animal. This little critter does something no other animal does. During a forest fire, echidnas will bury themselves as deep as they can, fall sleep, and wait for the flames to blow over. Instead of running, flying, or escaping like every other animal does when a forest fire strikes, the echidna is as cool as a cucumber; it just chills, patiently waiting for the fire to run its course.

Source: pelooyen/Adobe Stock

Echidnas are completely unfazed by the blazing flames. Their bodies literally go into a state of chilling, called *torpor*. This causes them to lower their body temperature, mental activity, and physical exertion and in turn enter a lethargic, life-preserving state.

Echidnas not only *survive* the forest fire, they actually end up *thriving in it*. Their incredible ability to go in and out of the torpor state enables them to turn their metabolism on and off at will. (Oh, what a superpower that would be for humans!)

Once the fire subsides, the echidna's former home will most likely be gone and their past completely burned; but they keep moving forward, baby step after baby step.

You are the echidna. As fiery as your past might be, as debilitating as it might seem, you are not defined by the fires you survive.

"We create our future, by well improving present opportunities; however few and small they are."

—Lewis Latimer

CHAPTER 3

The Inopportune

MEET SYBIL LUDINGTON

Sybil Ludington had no interest observing from the sidelines. Not now, not ever. Even at 16, the curious teenager was equipped with more gumption and direction than half the men she encountered—a trait her father, Colonel Henry Ludington, was particularly unfond of.

"Sybil, get in here this minute, young lady!" he roared from the next room. Towering over six feet, Henry was a no-nonsense New York militia officer working closely under the command of General George Washington.

"What did I tell you about keeping your nose outta other folks' business? Town hall meetings are no place for women. Your mother needs your help here, around the house."

The year was 1777. America had declared its independence the year prior, and Great Britain was in full attack. Even as a teenager, Sybil possessed a burning desire in her heart to contribute in any way she could.

"But, Dad," she pleaded.

"Don't you 'but, Dad' me, girl. I told you where you need to be, and you damn sure better be there next time."

Sybil's chest billowed defeatedly. She knew no one could ignore the other side of an argument better than her father. Disagreeing was pointless. After all, she was only 16. A fact her father reminded her of incessantly. "It's just a number," Sybil thought. Just a number.

She knew deep down she could help on the battlefield, that she was capable of more. If only her father would let her.

At every town hall meeting, the New York area leaders came together to strategize how to hold off the British. When the great George Washington would come to town, he confided in Sybil's father.

Sybil, the oldest of 12 siblings, had been tasked with looking after her younger brothers and sisters. They lived on a farm with acreage, and planting season was right around the corner.

But Sybil *hated* planting season.

"Sybil, can you please help your brother in the field today?" her mother called from the kitchen, stirring a hot pot of porridge.

"He needs your help. These mouths aren't going to feed themselves, ya know." Sybil reluctantly obliged, moping as she made her way out to the fields to help her brother scatter seeds for the upcoming harvest.

As she trudged through the field, thoughts filled her mind. "You can be a hero, Sybil. Who says you can't because you are too young?"

"Hey, get your backside over here, sis. This sun ain't goin'ta stay up all day long!"

Days were predictable in the small Danbury, Connecticut, community. Life was good; life was peaceful.

Even though they were in the midst of a revolutionary war, the attacks from the British had subsided in recent months. Yes, they still needed to be on guard, but the pressure of imminent invasion was no longer at the forefront of their minds.

Sybil could still dream. Later that day as she mounted her horse, Star, she envisioned strolling together in a parade to celebrate her bravery and honor. "Sybil Ludington, a war hero." She could hear the crowd cheering now.

"Sybil," her father yelled, ripping her from her reverie. "If I've told you once, I've told you a million times, you're too young to ride the horse into town. And what are you going into town for anyways? You're supposed to stay here and look after your younger brothers and sisters."

There it was again. *Too young.* Too young to be who she was ready to be, too young to make a difference. "Well, when is the right time?" Sybil muttered under her breath as she hopped off Star and marched inside, slamming the door behind her.

One day she'd be old enough to ride alone; one day she'd be old enough to go to town meetings; one day she'd be a hero! One day. But not today. Today, she was too young.

Then came April 26, 1777. A day as gloomy as the sky. Her father had traveled into town earlier that day for a town hall meeting, leaving her at home, forced to count raindrops for entertainment.

Suddenly, the front door flung open. "They're coming!" her father hollered. Every fiber of Sybil's being tensed. "Who?" she asked. "The British! They're going to burn down Danbury! You must all take shelter." For a moment, Sybil was paralyzed with fear. "Go!" he ordered, snapping her into motion.

An exhausted messenger had arrived at the town hall with news of the imminent attack on Danbury, which was about 15 miles away and where the munitions of the Continental Army's militia of the entire region were located. The British had 2,000 men actively aiming to destroy the arms and ammunition stockpile. Sybil's father needed to round up and assemble his militia of 400 men and act fast.

"But all the men are back home tending to their fields; there's no way to get ahold of them," Sybil's mother said, face white as a ghost. "You'll never be able to reach them in time."

Sybil knew the lives of thousands of people were in her father's hands and slowly slipping through his fingertips.

"Sybil, I need you. Are you ready?" her father asked quietly, knowing he could be delivering his daughter a death sentence.

"What are you talking about father?" she sputtered, confused, but knowing he was about to ask something very important of her.

"I need you to ride through the countryside and alert every one of my men that the British are going to burn down Danbury and that we need to band together to form our troops. I have to stay home to formulate a plan and await the men's arrivals. I know I have always told you that you are too young, but you are the only one capable right now of spreading the word. Can you do it?"

Sybil registered the concern in her father's eyes. The desperation, the fear. In that moment, she knew she was their only hope.

THE CRUX

Does Sybil take her dad's orders and ride through the night alerting the greater New York area of the oncoming attack? Or does she listen to the voices she's heard her entire life: "you're too young"?

***

Timing is everything. Or is it?

Is there actually a right time, a perfect time? Are we meant to wait until our number is called? Or do we take action and by doing so prompt the phone to ring?

Procrastination, a word that holds so much weight and meaning, is also a word we have the power to define. Sure, some studies show people who procrastinate can perform better when the pressure is on and the shot clock is winding down. And it sounds sexy to be that person, but is that really you? A very small handful yes, but you? Probably not.

Procrastination is derived from the ancient Greek word *akrasia*, meaning to do something against your better judgment. Procrastination is not actually a time management problem; it is an emotion regulation problem. In a 2013 study, Dr. Timothy Pychyl and Dr. Fuschia Sirois found procrastination can be best understood as "the primacy of short-term mood repair . . . over the longer-term pursuit of intended actions." Put simply, procrastination is more about finding immediate relief from a negative feeling than intentionally putting off long-term tasks. Procrastination is a set of buzzer-beater Band-Aids that hide the Peter Pan wound of never wanting to grow up and focus on the long term.

So why does our propensity to procrastinate continually distract us from taking greater action? A closer look at how our brain and heart work will explain.

The Brain

Our brains are designed to sustain our survival. Even if we know that putting off a task in the present will lead to more stress and anxiety in the future, our brains are wired to be more concerned with removing the immediate threat in the present. This is what is called the *amygdala hijack*.

This hijack leaves us paralyzed—we fail to take action, rationalizing we should wait for a "better time" or "perfect age."

Enter the game changer: neuroplasticity. Our brain can adapt as a result of experiences. Plasticity refers to the brain's malleability, which is defined as being easily influenced, trained, or controlled.

Neuroplasticity changes everything we believe when it comes to "the right age." The human brain is composed of nearly 100 billion neurons. When we are young, our brain tends to be more sensitive and responsive to experiences than our older brains are. The synapses in our neurons fire at a higher rate because we are exposed to many more new experiences early in our life. But this does not mean adult brains are not capable of adaptation. Plasticity is ongoing throughout life and can increase as a response to learning, experiences, and memory formation.

Sure, we can learn a language much easier when we are 5 than when we are 65, but that doesn't mean we can't; the plasticity in our brain allows us to ace the Spanish final even when we are 95!

One of the greatest lies society wants us to believe is that our brain stops developing at a certain age. Technically our brain stops *maturing* in our late twenties. But *maturing* and *learning* are two very different words.

Another very dangerous word in the English language is the explosive word *potential*, which means having or showing the capacity to become or develop into something in the future. But what potential actually means is *absolutely nothing*.

Potential has no substance before actualization. Until then, it's merely a lie we tell ourselves to make us feel better about who we'll be someday instead of who we are today. For example, when someone dubs us as having potential, something inside us blindly accepts the belief that one day in the future we will become this person, this *potential self* others say we will eventually be. The only problem is, there is no vehicle for this ride, no sherpa waiting to carry us to the top of our Mt. Everest.

There are two ends to the *potential spectrum*: the side where your younger self waits eagerly for the phone to ring and the side where your older self jadedly wonders why the phone never rang.

The phone of potential only rings if you make the call.

If you allow it, your self-perception of age will become a self-fulfilling prophecy. Before we go any further, please understand this. Your age isn't an excuse. Your age isn't a limitation. Your age is an advantage! I repeat: your age is an *advantage*. Whether you think you are too young or you think you are too old, you're not. Your brain is able to take on new challenges and be transformed at any age. It doesn't matter if you are 16 or 60, you are exactly where you should be in life.

Was Nola Ochs, from Jetmore, Kansas, too old when she graduated college at age 95? Was Alexander the Great too young to lead thousands into battle and conquer countries when he was just 18 years old?

Age is what you decide it to be; action is *when* you decide it to be.

The Heart

We live in a catch-22 society. We are never told there is a *right time*. Yet we look at the routes others have paved before us, and we either think one of two things: my time will come or my time has passed.

If you are too young, you believe no one is going to take you seriously. If you are too old, you believe you will just be left on the outside of the cool club looking in.

There never is a *right time* to take action, there never has been, and there never will be. Once you understand that, you can shed the notion of "waiting" for the right time.

Trust me, you will always be too old or too young if you think you are. Our hearts run on hope. Hope for our future.

In 2008, doctors Denise R. Bieke, Keith D. Markman, and Figen Kardogan studied the future opportunity principle and the lost opportunity principle. Their work suggests people mostly regret lost opportunities that they no longer have the chance to change. Future opportunities, however, enable people to envision various outcomes, which they have the power to create. This increases feelings of hope and reduces feelings of regret. Lost opportunities make it difficult for people to achieve psychological closure because they can no longer change the undesired outcome.

They argue that—no matter a person's age—future opportunities will provide future hope.

Meaning, if our hearts can anticipate possibilities in the future, that sense of hope makes us more likely to take action, regardless of our age.

The heart's main job is to keep you out of harm's way. And the most self-preserving excuse you can tell yourself in the present time is the notion that it just isn't your time right now. After using this excuse, the heart feels reassured and comfortable, making it the ideal go-to excuse moving forward. Then, the more you permit yourself to make these excuses, the more you feel okay about your inaction because you believe it "isn't your time."

But by living only in the present, without a vision for your future, you are cutting off any possibility of making your future self a reality. This is what is known as *temporal self-discontinuity*.

Psychologist Hal Hershfield, a professor of marketing at the UCLA Anderson School of Management, found that human beings perceive their future selves more like strangers than as part of their actual selves. Seeing is believing, when believing should be seeing.

The disconnect between your present and future selves can cause you to procrastinate for many different reasons. For example, you delay making healthy diet changes because you can't see the present ramifications that eating poorly has on your body. Your thinking sounds a bit like this: "I don't need to worry about the future, my future self will take care of any consequences that are to come. I just need to live in the moment. My present self doesn't have to worry about getting things done, that's the responsibility of my future self!"

That is very dangerous thinking. Yes, you do want to be present, but you can't only live in the present. This type of thinking causes you to live in a reactive life state instead of a creative life state. But only one person makes that choice: you.

The choice is yours. Are you going to use timing as an excuse for why you aren't where you want to be?

Are you too young?

Are you too old?

If you believe you are, then you are.

WHAT ACTUALLY HAPPENED TO SYBIL LUDINGTON?

On that April night in 1877, 16-year-old Sybil Ludington took action. She took her father's orders and mounted Star, her loyal steed. It was already 9 pm, pitch dark, with dim moonlight and starlight to guide her rainy ride. But Sybil would not be deterred from her mission. Sybil took off from her family's farm in Kent. She rode throughout the entirety of Putnam County, New York, south to Mahopac, west to Mahopac Falls, north to Kent Cliffs and Farmers Mills, and then even further north to Stormville.

Even though potential danger loomed around every corner, she kept going. The eyes of the British could be on her back at any moment with their muskets ready to strike if they spotted her. But Sybil didn't care; she put her life on the line to deliver the message.

As she rode through the shadowed countryside, she yelled at the top of her lungs, "The British are coming! The British are burning Danbury!" Her bold message rallied more than 400 Colonial militia men to assemble, nearly the entire regiment of the region. All in all, Sybil covered 40 miles, twice the distance and under much harsher conditions than that of the famed Paul Revere ride.

Sybil sparked a movement. Her efforts drove General William Tyron and his British troops back to their boats on Long Island Sound, preventing their advance into New York and protecting many more American towns from being attacked. This wasn't the only by-product of Sybil's midnight ride. The threat to Danbury also led to a surge of Patriot support as 3,000 more local Connecticut residents joined the Army of Reserve to protect the young nation.

Sybil was later thanked for her heroism by General George Washington. While she relished the national recognition and her new-found status as a local hero, her father's words were what she cherished the most: "You're never too young to be who God created you to be."

FLIP THE SCRIPT

Now let's imagine what it would look like if Sybil Ludington had never taken action because she believed she was too young to jump on her horse and alert the countryside of Britain's impending invasion.

You wake up this morning, brush your teeth, take a shower, and walk down the stairs to start the day. Anticipating the coffee and breakfast your husband always makes you in the morning, you think it's *just another Tuesday.*

As you sit down at the table, you glance at the finance section of the newspaper and notice the value of the British pound has dropped. You don't think much of it; it must be a focus on international finance today.

Your husband walks into the room carrying a tray with your coffee and breakfast on it. He carefully places the plate on the table so as to not break the fine china.

"Fine china?" you think. Where is your favorite sports team mug? You take a sip of your coffee and quickly spit it out. "Phwwwww! What is this?" You demand half shocked, half angered.

"It's your tea, dear. You drink it every morning." Your confused husband responds in a thick British accent.

You now look down at your breakfast. Baked beans, roasted tomato, and a crumpet. "What on God's green earth is going on here?" you think to yourself.

You scramble quickly to check the newspaper you had glanced at earlier. That wasn't international finance you were looking at, that was *the* finance section.

"Who is the president," you ask your husband, beginning to panic.

He is dumbfounded. "President? What is that?" clearly thinking you have lost it.

"The leader of the free world! Our great country of America!" you exclaim about ready to lose it.

"King William III is our leader, my dear; you know that," your husband says, now resting his hand on your upper back as if to offer condolences to your kookiness.

There is no United States of America. There is no president, there is no free speech, there is no freedom like you thought you knew. The British conquered young America in the American Revolution, and there was one battle that marked the turning point of the war: The Battle for Danbury. Sybil Ludington never saddled up her horse that night. She doubted herself, resolving instead that she could never do something meaningful at the age of 16. She was always told she was too young, and she believed it. She didn't ride 40 miles through the New York countryside alerting the troops of the British invasion. All was lost because she accepted that it just "wasn't her time."

There will never be a *right time* to take action. You'll always be able to make the excuse that you are too young, or too old, or that the time just isn't yours. A person can go their entire life without anyone challenging that narrative, and be okay. But *okay* isn't what you were made for. God didn't create you to just be *okay*. He created you to strive for your greatness, no matter how young or how old you might be.

You might think you are too young to start a company that actualizes an idea you believe will help improve millions of lives. You might think you are too old to make a career change because your time has passed you by. You might think the time just isn't *your time* now and continue to wait for the phone to ring. You'll be waiting for years hoping someone spoon-feeds you the life you dream of living. But I have news for you. That proverbial phone will never ring; you have to pick up the phone and make the call!

The idea of change is daunting no matter what age you are. The reason change is scary is because it is an emotional experience. It signifies the end of something that was once a known commodity in your life. But did you know that changing isn't the daunting task you actually fear. The *transition* is. Transitioning is the difficult part that your brain and heart want to avoid.

Transition is the actual *resistance*. Transition is the *fear of the unknown*.

Transition is the "What if I don't measure up?" "What if I fail?" "What if I look stupid in front of my peers?" Transition is the *what-if fears*.

No matter your age, you can make a difference in your life and the lives of others. You can start today! Here's how.

Tools to Overcome the Inopportune

"You can time the stock market just right."

"Wait for the right time before proposing."

"You'll know when the right time to ask for a raise is."

"Just wait for your time, the door will open for you."

Said no successful person in the history of ever. Procrastination sounds cool, and sure it's en vogue these days. But the only thing "en" about it is that it will "end" your dreams.

Tell me if you want to procrastinate after reading this study: Piers Stell at the University of Calgary, widely recognized as one of the top procrastination researchers throughout the world, found that after reviewing hundreds of studies an overwhelming 94% of the people surveyed said procrastination *hurt* their happiness. Additionally, employees who procrastinate keep worrying about work long after they've left the office. Students who procrastinate receive lower course grades, lower overall grades, and lower exam scores. If that wasn't enough, procrastination is also strongly linked to poor health and powerfully coordinated to poor financial health.

Ideas without action is procrastination in a bottle. Everyone has an idea. Ideas are worth nothing until action is put toward the idea. Ideas are worth a penny, action is worth a million bucks. And the only way to ensure you don't become one of the *procrastinators* is to set daily staples of discipline. Discipline equals freedom. Procrastination and blaming your age equals, well, nothing. Literally nothing.

You know *why* you are the inopportune; now it's time for me to show you how to conquer this archetype.

The NOW Alarm

Remember in high school when you learned about Newton's first law in science class? "An object at rest stays at rest and an object in motion stays in motion with the same speed and the same direction unless acted upon by an unbalanced force." The same thing can be applied to you.

Here is my take on Newton's law when it comes to action: "A person will not take action until that person is told to take action." This means you must build in the disruptions to set the *object* (you) *in motion*.

Our brain is constantly on autopilot, or what is known as default mode network (DMN). It was discovered in the early 1990s when researchers noticed that patients in brain scanners were still showing patterns of neurological activity even at rest.

Sure, taking advantage of our brain's autopilot mode has its time and place. For example: when you can have creative mind wandering while doing dishes or when you are able to engage in conversation with your spouse while simultaneously cooking dinner for her. Multitasking is a positive of autopilot.

But what happens when our brain's baseline state is *autopilot?* The short answer: you will wake up ten years from now wondering where the past ten years went and why you never took the chance of living a life of fulfillment.

The good news is, your baseline of life doesn't have to be on auto-pilot. You can turn procrastination into prioritization with one three-lettered alarm: NOW!

Procrastination has been linked directly to higher levels of stress, anxiety, frustration, guilt, and in some cases low self-esteem and depression. *Prioritization* has been linked to lower stress levels, increased productivity, higher energy throughout the day, more motivation, and ample time to relax anxiety-free.

Action step for today: Create an alarm on your phone titled "the NOW alarm." Set the NOW alarm for noon, and set it to repeat daily. (Of course, set it for a different time if you know you are going to be in a meeting or on a call at noon that day.)

The point of the NOW alarm is to alert your mind to take action *now*. Not later, not tomorrow, NOW!

The great news is that it only takes five minutes a day to ensure that you are living a life of prioritization over one of procrastination. With your alarm now set, open a Notes folder on your phone (or whatever way you most commonly take notes) and write down the three questions I list next. Save this note so you are able to easily come back to it every day when the NOW alarm goes off midday. When the alarm goes off, ask yourself these three questions:

- What is the one most important thing I can do *right now* that will move the needle in my life and help improve the lives of others?

- What am I currently putting off that if I take action on will provide me with more peace?

- Who could I send a quick message of genuine encouragement to that might spark them to take action?

Don't wait until tomorrow to set your NOW alarm; do it right NOW!

Others Have Done It, So Can You

There are very few things that have never been accomplished before. That's just the truth. You can either look at that statement with disdain and wish you could teleport back to the 1980s and invent the internet, or you can look at that statement with the mindset "if they can do it, then so can I!"

There is a lot of confidence to be gained through knowing someone has paved the trail before you. You don't have to be the first to venture through the dangerous jungle to find the paradise beach. The footsteps have already been walked in, the roadblocks have already been pushed aside, and now you can take those same great steps forward.

Think you are too young to achieve anything great? Think again.

Louis Braille was 15 when he created the language of Braille.

Laura Dekker was 14 when she sailed around the world solo.

Bobby Fischer was 15 when he became a Chess Grandmaster.

Alexander the Great was 16 when he founded his first colony.

Joan of Arc was 19 when she stood up for her entire country.

Jordan Romero was 13 when he scaled Mt. Everest.

Mark Zuckerberg was 19 when he founded Facebook.

Wolfgang Mozart was 8 when he wrote his first symphony.

Malala Yousafzai was 17 when she won the Nobel Peace Prize.

Blaise Pascal was 19 when he developed the calculator.

Think you are too old to achieve anything great? Try telling that to . . .

Julia Child, who was 50 when she published her first cookbook

Ray Croc, who was 52 when he founded McDonald's System Inc.

Samuel L. Jackson, who was 43 when he finally landed a major role in a movie

Colonel Sanders, who was 65 when he started Kentucky Fried Chicken

Laura Ingalls Wilder, who was 65 when she started writing *Little House on the Prairie*

Gladys Burrill, who was 86 when she began her marathon running career

Charles Darwin, who was 50 when he published his *Theory of Evolution*

Greatness doesn't care how old you are.

Greatness doesn't discriminate against the young or the old.

Greatness doesn't make excuses that it "isn't the right time."

Greatness is greatness, and it is yours for the taking. If, and only if, you take action!

Action tool: In your action notebook (or whatever form of journaling you choose), write down the following:

- Three people in your life or famous people you aspire to be like who were considered "too young"

- Three people in your life or famous people you aspire to be like who were considered "too old"

Mark this page in your notebook so you are easily able to come back to it at any time when you feel you are "too young" or "too old."

Bonus points for continuing to build out the list of "too young" and "too old" people in your life.

Now write your name below this paragraph (physically in the book) and then write the words MY TIME IS NOW directly under your name. This is a contract with yourself to NEVER allow age to play a factor in whether you can take action or not. Take a picture of this contract and save it to your phone. You now have contractual proof if you ever catch yourself thinking you are "too young" or "too old."

YOUR ACTION ANIMAL: THE THOROUGHBRED RACEHORSE

The greatest athletes, arguably on the planet, don't run up and down the basketball court; they don't sprint from end to end on the soccer pitch; they don't even leap for touchdowns in the back of the football field endzone.

Nope, they race around a dirt track. (Sorry, NASCAR fans, I'm not talking about you.)

I'm talking about thoroughbred racehorses. Secretariat, Man-O-War, and Seabiscuit. The names of these great thoroughbreds will live forever in sports history. Michael Jordan was 28 when he won his first NBA title. These horses? They were only three years old.

Source: Lukas Gojda/Adobe Stock

Is it just me or does that sound really young?

Imagine a three-year-old toddler going head to head with Jordan's 1998 Chicago Bulls. Yeah, that might not turn out so well for the youngster.

Technically, a thoroughbred horse doesn't reach its full maturity and racing potential until a few years later. And I know what you are thinking, "a horse doesn't live as long as a human." True, I get that. But three years is still three years; the number of days lived is the exact same.

A three-year-old thoroughbred is still gaining its competitive racing legs, inexperienced, underdeveloped, but yet thrown into the starting gate of one of the world's biggest money-driven sports known to people.

You might not think you're ready for your calling; you might not think you are old enough to even get in the game. If you wait until the game starts, you will never be ready to actually play it. You must start acting like the game is *now*. Throw yourself onto the track and run! Your older self will thank your younger *thoroughbred* self that you did. Secretariat was less than 1,000 days old when he won the Triple Crown and shattered all horse racing speed records. You were most likely still in diapers when you were 1,000 days old.

But just because most thoroughbreds are young when they rise to dominance, don't for a second think the "old" thoroughbreds can't leave a legacy.

The racehorse Al Jabal was 19 years old when he won The Three Handicap Stakes, a highly touted race in the United Kingdom. This was 16 years older than the "normal" age champions.

On top of that, elderly thoroughbreds arguably live the best life of any creature on the planet. They become what is known as a broodmare or stud, living the remainder of their years on lush, green breeding grounds. Basically translated: "big man on campus on the best campus in the country."

Embrace the thoroughbred you are and take action, NOW! In the end, Sybil knew she was meant for greatness. And not just greatness, but significance. Despite the naysayers in her life, she believed she was capable of fulfilling her potential in the present moment. Not someday in the future, not when she was "old enough," but now.

Your potential doesn't care what year you were born. It doesn't care if you're too young to vote or too old to do a cartwheel. It doesn't care if you have one too many grey hairs or one too few life experiences. Accept your potential today. Let it quench your thirst, satisfy your soul, and propel you toward your wildest dreams.

Not tomorrow, not next week, not when you finish this or finish that, but now.

Right.

Now.

Others have done it, so can you!

"Then, who is my messenger to be?"
Said Sybil Ludington, "You have me."
"You!" said the Colonel, and grimly smiled.
"You!" My daughter, you're just a child!"
"Child!" cried Sybil. "Why I'm sixteen!
My mind's alert and my senses keen,
I know where the trails and the roadways are
And I can gallop as fast and as far
As any masculine rider can.
You want a messenger? I'm your man!"
                                   —Poem by Berton Braley

CHAPTER 4

The Blamer

MEET WILMA RUDOLPH

Stairs. Wilma hated stairs. Almost as much as she hated her leg. Just the one. The other was fine. It was nothing special, but at least it did what it was meant to do. But not her left leg. Nope. The left one, Wilma loathed. No one else in her family had to wear a clunky brace or be carried up the stairs. Nothing about her siblings garnered unwanted looks everywhere they went. Two working legs. Was that so much to ask?

"Get this off of me!" seven-year-old Wilma screamed from the bedroom she shared with two of her sisters.

"You can't get it off! You won't be able to go with us if you do," her older sister responded as if Wilma was crazy.

"I'm not going to the movie theater. I hate my leg!" Wilma sobbed laying on her bed.

The movie theater meant stairs. And lots of them. A bumpy terrain her unstable frame failed to conquer on its own time and time again. She had no interest facing that humiliating dragon ever again.

Good fortune was not a term one would associate with Wilma Rudolph. Born prematurely on June 23, 1940, in St. Bethlehem, Tennessee, Wilma weighed a frail 4½ pounds. She was the 20th of 22 children. But fighting for the attention of her parents was the least of her worries. As a young child, she fought through measles, mumps, and chicken pox. When she was four years old, she nearly died after contracting double pneumonia and scarlet fever simultaneously.

By six years old, she was a survivor of polio. But the virus left her leg paralyzed, forcing her to rely on a leg brace she hated more than anything.

She was not even able to compete with her siblings for the dibs on dinner; Wilma became accustomed to cold leftovers. "Wilma, I'm coming, deary. Don't you cry now," Blanche Rudolph, Wilma's mother, hollered from the kitchen.

"It's okay dear, it's okay. Mama's got you." Blanche took off Wilma's brace and began massaging her foot, as she did multiple times per day, attempting to regenerate blood flow throughout her paralyzed limb.

"Mama, why can't I just be normal? Why can't I walk like everyone else?" Wilma asked.

"My dear Wilma, you are normal. Your foot's a long ways from your heart. And boy do you have a beautiful heart," her mother assured her, bringing Wilma's head close to her chest while stroking her hair.

Wilma needed special medical attention—attention her family couldn't afford. The Rudolphs were anything but wealthy. And growing up in the 1940s and 1950s as an African American in the United States didn't cut Wilma any breaks. The only hospitals nearby were for white people, and the Rudolphs didn't have a car to take to other cities.

"Freak!"

"Cripple!"

The people in town were ruthless, shouting jabs at Wilma as she hobbled to church each Sunday morning. Unable to move quickly, she would try her best to drown out the insults, with her heart lower than her feet. "If only I had a normal leg!!" was a thought that ran on replay through Wilma's mind. Biting her lower lip, she fought back bitter tears. "I'll never be normal! I'll never fit in. I'll never be able to even stand to sing in the church choir! My family is too poor. My leg is a curse! Why me, God?!" She couldn't hold back the tears any longer as they welled up in her eyes.

"I'm so sorry, dear," her mother consoled her as they sat in the back pew together.

"I promise you'll walk one day," Blanche continued as she stretched out her arms to Wilma.

Wilma turned her head and refused the impending hug. "Mama, I want to run like the other kids at school. I want to show them I can do it and that I'm faster than every single last one of them," Wilma said with determination while wiping tears from her cheeks.

Wilma spent the next few years going through the motions. She was quiet, shy, and reclusive. A shell of the bubbly, optimistic young child she once was. Desperate to reignite the spark that once radiated through Wilma, her mother tracked down a specialist who eventually agreed to give Wilma physical therapy. Because the family didn't have a car, Wilma's mother found a public bus to transport them. Every week, Wilma and her mother traveled 100 miles round trip to the closest hospital that treated Black people, Meharry Medical College in Nashville.

After years of treatment, and daily leg massaging help from her older siblings, Wilma began to act like her former self. She walked without her brace, all by herself. Cheers filled the hallway, as her family and doctors celebrated the massive accomplishment. Everyone was jubilant, but Wilma's joy was fleeting. If finding and maintaining your balance at 12 months old is normal, then successfully shuffling a few steps down a hall at 12 years old must be the exact opposite.

Abnormal.

"What is there to celebrate about that?" Wilma thought.

On the morning of Wilma's 13th birthday, she woke with a numbness. Every birthday was the same. No gifts, no decorations, no fanfare. The family simply couldn't afford it. Why would this birthday be any different?

"Happy birthday, sweetie," her family said in unison. Wilma couldn't believe her eyes. A gift? For her? "Go on, open it," her mom encouraged her. Wilma took the box and slowly peeled it open.

In an instant, her eyes moistened. A special orthopedic shoe rested inside.

"You don't have to wear that clunky old boot anymore, dear; we got you this special shoe. You'll be able to walk to church in it, play sports in it, even go on a date with that Eldridge boy you have your eye on," Wilma's mother said with a teasing smile.

A blush marched up Wilma's cheeks. Wilma was still extremely self-conscious but she had a smile on her face her mother had not seen in years.

Wilma wore the shoe to school the next day, hoping Robert Eldridge would take notice. And as a Cinderella glass slipper story would have it, Robert not only took notice, but he asked her out on a date for that Friday.

"Wilma, would you do me the honor of having dinner at the A & W Motor court with me this Friday?" Robert asked nervously awaiting a response.

"I, I would. Yes, I would like that." Wilma responded sheepishly. "I'll see you there at seven."

Friday seemed lightyears away. And when Wilma strolled to the local A & W, about a quarter mile from her house, she saw Robert standing out front, a smile stretching from ear to ear.

"Why, hello there, Wilma, you look quite nice tonight," Robert said as he opened the door for Wilma.

Seated in the restaurant booth, Robert and Wilma talked for hours. The dinner couldn't have gone better and Robert offered to escort Wilma home, being the thoughtful gentleman he was.

Just as Wilma approached the front door, Robert softly grabbed her hand. Wilma turned her head, knowing exactly why he had stopped her. Nerves taking hold, she attempted to turn her body so she could lean in for the kiss. But instead of smoothly planting her foot and landing the turn, her leg gave out from underneath her. In what felt like slow motion, Wilma collapsed to the pavement, sufficiently ruining the moment. It was over. Once again, the leg she hated so deeply, had ruined everything.

"I will never be normal," Wilma muttered between sobs and sniffles as Robert hoisted her back on her feet and sat her down on the front porch.

"Sure you will, Wilma," Robert tried to convince her.

Once inside, Wilma's mother wiped the tears from her eyes; She had been spying from the kitchen window and had seen what happened. "Momma, I'll never get to do the things I want to do. I'll never be normal!"

Normal to Wilma was just a fantasy.

***

"Basketball tryouts are today after school," Wilma's history teacher announced loudly as class was being dismissed the following Monday. "If you would like to try out, proceed to the gymnasium after school and I and the other coaches will select the team."

"Basketball is the last thing I want to do." Wilma thought as she heard her teacher make the announcement. "Besides, even if I did, it's not like I ever could."

As she sullenly grabbed her backpack and headed for the hallway door, she stopped when she heard her name.

"Wilma?" Her teacher said rather loudly to make sure he got her attention.

"I'm the girls' basketball coach this year, and I could really use an athlete with your height out there. Can you run on that leg?" He asked, not trying to crush the wind in her sails but wanting to be realistic with her.

The painful memories of all the times her leg failed her flashed through her head. The pity glances, the snickers, the endless parade of soul-sucking almost. Basketball? How could he possibly suggest something of her that was so clearly impossible?

"So, what do you say?" He asked, cutting to the chase. "You wanna try out or what?"

THE CRUX

Does Wilma put her blaming mindset on the sidelines and try out for the basketball team risking ridicule, scorn, and judgment from her peers? Or does she decide not to and continue to live her life in a safe bubble, continuing to blame her circumstances, her parents, and God?

***

Point your index finger at someone else. Now, how many of your fingers are pointing back at you? Are you someone who is naturally inclined to blame someone or something before taking ownership yourself? Do you look for excuses or look for solutions?

To find out, ask yourself these questions:

- Do you think your current situation is the result of someone else's mishaps?

- Is there something or someone in the past that has unfairly left you at a disadvantage?

- When you read this sentence does a response quickly pop into your mind: If only _____, then I would be able to _____.

- When was the last time you directed blame onto someone else to make yourself look better in front of your peers? Or even to feel better about yourself when you are alone? If you're being honest, it was probably today. Maybe even a couple of times.

Blaming is rooted in your personal need for self-validation. It's ego, it's fear, it's a free pass from ever having to take responsibility. But where does this blaming mentality come from and how does it hold you back from taking action?

To first figure out why you blame, we must get to the root cause: the past. Now, this is different from being burned by the past and afraid of being burned again. What I'm referring to is using something unfortunate or limiting in your past as an excuse for why you can't accomplish something now. The circumstances around this past event or person might be 100% *not* your fault; however, you now use this as a crutch throughout your life and allow it to affect 100% of your life choices.

Let's start with the way you were raised. If this doesn't stir up the emotional blaming, I don't know what will. Did your folks sabotage your life in some way? Was your dad insensitive and uncommunicative? Was your mom selfish and prone to self-medicating? Did they favor your sibling more? Skip your sporting events or your dance competitions? Did they divorce, forcing you to lose faith in love and relationships? Were they overworked? Underpaid? Abusive?

Blaming your parents for your less-than-savory traits is easy. Why wouldn't you follow in their footsteps? Feeling tainted by your genes is nothing new. Our parents and childhood have a massive effect on who we are and the way we are. Whether it's your mom and dad, or a teacher, coach, family member, neighbor, friend, bully, town, city, state, school, teammate, accident, illness, injury, rejection . . . finding someone or something in your past to blame will continue to destroy you if you let it.

The Brain

The observations and interactions you experience during childhood condition your brain to form your *blamer scale*. Your opinions and beliefs are based on what you *think* is happening. Your experiences and perceptions shape your reality, causing subjective thought patterns to fire throughout the neurological network of the brain. This is called *cognitive bias*. A cognitive bias is a subconscious error in thinking that leads you to misinterpret information from the world around you and affects the rationality and accuracy of decisions and judgments.

Here's an example: you didn't get the job because the other candidate has a prominent father. Your father's name has never helped you get into any room in the past; in fact, it may have even kept you out of a few. Automatically, you create a seemingly logical explanation in your mind: "Well, I didn't even stand a chance. Her father got her that job. If only I had a more prominent father." This narrative becomes entrenched in your brain, resurfacing quickly for future blaming use.

The next time you are up for a job and don't get it, your first assumption is the competing candidate was born with one foot already in the door. You begin to see similar "unfair" situations play out in all different sectors of your life—not because they are actually occurring *more*, but instead because your awareness of the occurrence has heightened, due to your *cognitive bias* (aka blaming).

What you don't have isn't your fault, right? (That's a rhetorical question.) When operating in neutral, your mind defaults to highlighting the things you *don't have*, as opposed to the things you do. It turns out you're neurologically predisposed to blame your situation on what you don't have. From the early days of human existence, any weaknesses or disadvantages caused people to prepare defense mechanisms. It is why our fight-or-flight senses are naturally much stronger than our "everything is going to be okay" senses when challenging situations arise.

When something isn't going your way, do you first try to think of an alternative solution, or do you automatically blame something outside of your environmental control? The blaming mentality is the core reason we live in a "give up when things don't go my way" society.

According to Saul McLeod, "Neuroscientific evidence has shown that there is greater neural processing in the brain in response to negative stimuli." That's very interesting when you think about it. Your brain works hardest when it is receiving negative stimuli.

In studies conducted by psychologist John Cacioppo, participants were shown pictures of either positive, negative, or neutral images. Negative images produced much stronger electrical activity in the cerebral cortex (information processor) than positive or neutral images.

So why does it make sense to focus on what you don't have and force your brain to work even harder than it has to? It doesn't. But yet, we are conditioned to do so.

This response to negative stimuli begins at a very young age, as early as three months old. Incredible! You don't come into this world with negative biases, but even only three months into your existence you are already applying more meaning to your negative experiences. Not your fault, the world's fault, right? Well, only if you see it that way.

So now that we know the mind is more inclined to register the negative, let's go even more in-depth and see how it correlates with not taking action. In their work on heuristics and biases, Nobel Prize–winning researchers Daniel Kahneman and Amos Tversky found that when making decisions, people consistently place greater weight on negative aspects of an event than they do on positive ones. Meaning, if you are told to imagine one positive picture and one negative picture and then make an unrelated decision based solely on your feelings, the negative picture would most likely determine your decision.

This proclivity to the negative is an uphill battle you have to work to overcome. So if your mind is programmed to always lean toward the negative, it is easy to see why you are prone to believing others are to blame for your situation.

Do you find yourself blaming where you came from? If only you could have been born in a different city, a different state, or even a different country. If only you could have been born into a higher economic status. Into a different family. Things would be better. Have you found yourself mentally pointing a finger at someone, allowing an arbitrary excuse like where or how you were raised to determine your current situation?

- "I'll never be qualified! I come from a family that has been wronged time and time again."

- "I never had extravagant birthday parties or annual family vacations. I had to work a summer job to pay for school while all the other students enjoyed time at the lake or beach."

- "I was dealt an unfair hand of cards in life! Nothing ever went my way."

- "I'm from a small cornfield town, I wasn't made for a job in the big city. It's true, if only I had been born in Manhattan, then maybe I could."

Do you find yourself blaming your physical inadequacies?

- "My nose is too big. I'll never get a date."

- "I'm too short to play basketball."

- "I'm overweight. It runs in my family."

- "My hairline is receding. No one will hire me."

- "I want to be a dancer but I don't have a natural turnout."

- "I wish I was a different ethnicity. My future is restricted by my skin."

- "I want to be a public speaker but I have a stutter."

Do these self-conceived *blaming* excuses in your mind hold you back from taking action toward becoming the person you want to be? Yeah, they do.

But remember, what you perceive as a flaw doesn't have to be debilitating.

Ask yourself, if you're not where you want to be in life right now, what or whom are you blaming? Blaming is the easy way out, but it'll never provide the fulfillment you are searching for. Action will.

The Heart

Blaming, in its purest form, is essentially *emotional avoidance*. It's a defense mechanism created to help protect your self-esteem.

Pinpoint a specific moment in your life when things didn't go the way you wanted them to. Maybe it was a rejection, a missed opportunity, or a physical disadvantage. Maybe you blame your parent, a coach, poor timing, or a catastrophic event. Your heart wants to protect your feelings, and it wants to avoid future pain of that same level at any cost. So it learns that if it directs blame onto anyone or anything else other than yourself, it can soften the blow.

We all want to be right, but don't necessarily want to "do the right thing." There is a big difference between the two. If doing the right thing means having to take ownership, the price can be too high. However, if we convince ourselves that ownership is not ours for the taking, then we can feel good about "being right." And when ownership is lost, responsibility disappears, and the only person left to blame is anyone other than yourself.

Fundamental attribution error describes the type of blame in which a person draws conclusions based on another person's internal characteristics (e.g., their current mood or mannerisms) without considering outside explanations (e.g., what's going on in their personal life). So in instances where we exhibit this type of blame, instead of first considering we might be at fault, and if not, then considering showing grace toward the person in question for the circumstances they might be going through, we immediately jump to attacking their character first. You cast a blanket of blame on others for who you *think* they are instead of considering their unique situation.

Your boss obviously has it out for you; why would he ever promote you? Does he actually have it out for you, though? Or was the real reason he snapped at you because he has two sick children at home and his marriage is strained? We don't know what others are going through. Their personal circumstances outside the given situation could very well be the reason for their behavior toward you. I'm not making an excuse for mistreatment or bad behavior. Rather, I'm encouraging you to acknowledge that other people do make mistakes; just don't let those mistakes dictate your emotions. Your heart wants to provide a cushion for you to fall on. If your boss or someone else does something unfavorable in your eyes, it's easy to sink into blame mode. It's much easier to blame than it is to keep moving forward and trying again. It's also easier to blame than it is to look in the mirror and take responsibility. So every single time, before you automatically point the finger at someone else, first take a deep breath and ask yourself this question: "Am I to blame in any way for my situation?"

The reason it's so easy to point blame is because it's a one-sided court argument without any cross-examination. There isn't a judge to hold you accountable, or to tell you you're wrong; there is no defendant to offer up the other side of the story. You win every court case with yourself. However, there is only one person that you can never fool. Yourself.

By casting blame on something or someone else, you feel better because you've given yourself a viable excuse for *why* you can't take action. It's not your fault. It never has been, right?

Are you harboring blame toward someone or something that needs to be released before you can take action? How could you instead view your past, inadequacies, or disadvantages as something that has not only helped shape you into the person you are today but has prepared you for the action you long to take?

What Actually Happened to Wilma Rudolph?

As Wilma stood on the sidelines, she could feel her classmates' eyes land on her. One by one, the steady echo of bouncing balls trailed off, as the girl with the messed-up leg stole everyone's attention. What on earth is *she* doing here? The coach blew his whistle, cutting through the tension. "Everyone, take five warm-up laps around the gym," he shouted.

Wilma's initial strides were as uneasy as her nerves, but in her mind—orthopedic shoe or not—she told herself she could run as well as anyone. And it wasn't long before she actually could. Not only did Wilma make the high school basketball team, but she thrived. She became so good on the court, she was eventually asked to join the track team. This was a highly competitive sport that involved the last skill she ever thought she was capable of mastering. Running became her favorite pastime: track, field, cross-country. She was addicted in the best kind of way.

Wilma led Burt High School to a state championship (without her special shoe) where she was noticed by Ed Temple, the track and field coach for Tennessee State University, a historically Black university in Nashville. Ed saw her potential, asking her to be a member of their summer program for the Tigerbelles, an all-Black group of female runners who were renowned for their discipline and speed.

Wilma's talent stood out among the rest, and she became an unofficial leader of the team. Only 16 at the time, Wilma burst onto the national scene at a high school track meet in Seattle where she ran a time fast enough to qualify her for the 1956 Olympics in Melbourne, Australia. And there, she went on to win a bronze medal in the 4 × 100 m relay.

The once disabled 13-year-old girl who doubted if she would be able to run up and down a basketball court, let alone ever run in her life, was an Olympic medalist three years later.

Further obstacles, however, presented themselves. When she returned home from Melbourne to finish high school, she became pregnant. Raising a young child while training relentlessly, and all during a time period in which women participating in sports was frowned on, was quite the challenge. But it was a challenge Wilma was up for. She refused to let anything hold her back.

In 1960, Ed Temple was selected to be the coach for that year's US Olympic Track and Field team. Serendipitously, the two were once

again teamed up, and in Rome, Wilma achieved the once unthinkable. She won gold medals in the 100 m dash, the 200 m dash, and the 4 ×100 m relay.

It was the first time an American woman won three gold medals in the same Olympics; and on top of that, Wilma set world records in the 200 m dash and the relay.

She was soon labeled "the fastest woman in the world." The very limbs she thought would hold her back forever became the very things that propelled her into greatness.

Wilma didn't just leave her impact on the track, however. When she returned home from Rome, she used her stardom to take a stand for civil rights. She refused to attend the welcome home celebration planned by Tennessee's governor because the event would be segregated. Her protest made a difference. The parade and banquet in her honor became the first integrated event in her hometown of Clarksville. And she continued to fight for this cause in the city until all segregation laws were eradicated.

Standing for women's rights and civil rights, Wilma was the ultimate fighter. For Wilma, her legacy was simple: "I would be very sad if I was only remembered as Wilma Rudolph, the great sprinter. To me, my legacy is to be an example for the youth of America and to let them know they can be anything they want to be." Instead of living a life full of blame, Wilma took action.

FLIP THE SCRIPT

Now let's imagine what it would look like if Wilma Rudolph had never taken action and continued to blame her leg and others for her situation.

Summer is your favorite time of the year. And low and behold your favorite sporting event just so happens to be taking place this year in its four-year cycle, the Summer Olympics.

You walk inside from a hot morning walk through downtown Franklin, Tennessee, where you and your family live, 20 minutes south of Nashville. There's nothing better than the refreshing taste of lemonade in the summer. You gulp down your glass, grab a towel to wipe the sweat from your brow, and make your way into the living room to watch the day's events on the TV.

It's time for track and field, your favorite. "Could today get any better?" you think as you kick your feet up on the recliner chair that you plan to lounge in for the remainder of the morning and likely the entirety of the day.

Bob Costas announces on the NBC broadcast, "Up next, the men's 100 m final followed by the men's 4 × 400 m semis and the men's long jump." Odd they would have so many men's events back to back, but you don't think too much of it. You watch intently as Jamaica wins the 100 m, South Africa wins the relay, and Barbados leads in the long jump.

Suddenly you realize something doesn't seem right. Not only are there no female competitors, there are also no African American racers on the track. "This can't be," you think, now starting to become very concerned. You reach for your phone to search the upcoming Olympic events schedule. Scrolling through event after event, you find NBC is airing only men's.

"What?" You are beyond confused by now as your eyes dart back to the TV to see only white American athletes running around the track.

Wilma Rudolph never took action when she was 13, so she didn't try out for the basketball team. She decided to take the blaming route and used her circumstance as an excuse. And since she never played basketball, she never discovered her gift for running. Wilma's dominance on the track couldn't exist. Her record-setting three gold medals in one Olympics never happened. The worldwide popularity that she had brought to being a female, African American athlete in track in field never materialized. And most of all, she never made a stand for civil rights and the importance of desegregation in America.

Sure, I know you are thinking, there were already females competing in sports and other African American athletes as well. But when a meteor strikes, it isn't forgotten. Wilma was that meteor.

The word *impossible* ends with *possible*. It doesn't matter how you start, where you come from, or what your physical or mental limitations are; you absolutely can make an impact on this world. But if you live as a pawn in the blame game, you will never discover that person you could have become.

You might not have the ideal genes. You might not come from the wealthiest family. You're probably not the smartest person in the room. Odds are your upbringing wasn't always picture perfect. I know you have insecurities, I know you have self-doubt, and I know it's easy to point the finger and offload the blame elsewhere. I totally understand, I have been there many times before.

But remember, Wilma had these exact same thoughts, too. When these thoughts enter your mind, think of her. If Wilma Rudolph could overcome her situation and circumstances, then I truly believe that by all means, so can you!

TOOLS TO OVERCOME THE BLAME GAME

Why did *they* get the job?

Why do *they* get to live in the big house in the nice neighborhood?

Why do *they* seem to catch all the breaks and never have a worry in the world?

Why do *they* seem to have just risen to success overnight?

Sound familiar? When was the last time you had one of these thoughts? Or all of them? I have good news and good news.

> Good news 1: Don't envy others' success until you have walked a mile in their shoes. Meaning, we don't know what others had to go through behind the scenes to achieve the level we see them at publicly. The cliché saying "It takes ten years to become an overnight success" is cliché for a reason. Don't blame them for their success. Cheer on their success!

> Good news 2: If someone does rise to "quick success," they have not built the foundation and the deep roots for what it takes to sustain the level they are at. Don't blame them; they experienced a flash in the pan and likely one day they will wish they were where you are now. It all works out if you don't take the easy route, the crowded highway of blame. Take the road less traveled of responsibility, discipline, and consistency, and trust me you will get there.

Good news 3: Say this out loud: "I have NO sunk costs." The past isn't time wasted; it is experience and wisdom gained. Everything you want to place *blame* on has taught you a lesson. The question is, are you going to use that lesson as a positive for future growth or a negative for debilitating regression?

You know *why* you are the blamer; now it's time for me to show you how to conquer this archetype.

Compensation Theory

What if the actual reason you are *blaming* was the reason for your success? Alfred Adler, the founder of the school of individual psychology, created what is known as the *compensation theory*. Society tells us our weaknesses are flaws, holding us back from what we *could* be. Alder, however, introduced a new way of thinking. What if our perceived weaknesses and the reasons why we *can't* do something actually become the reasons why we *can?*

Is it sheer luck that the two greatest composers of all time, Bach and Beethoven, were both deaf? Is it a coincidence that Andrea Bocelli, who has arguably one of the greatest singing voices of all time, is blind? Absolutely not.

One of the smartest and most accomplished scientific minds of all time was Albert Einstein. But did you know that he was dyslexic? His dyslexia, which is something that most people would see as a huge disadvantage, actually contributed to his genius.

What if you viewed what you see as your "disability" as an "ability," to stand out from the rest of the world?

Action step for today: What is a "flaw" of yours? What is something you blame your parents for or something from your past you're unable to let go of? Is it your height, is it your IQ, is it your singing voice, is it the way you look, is it the way your parents treated you, is it where you were born, is it the food stamps you had to live off when you were younger? The list can go on and on. Once you have identified that flaw, that disadvantage, write it down.

Here's my example:

My father is 6'5". The doctor told me I would grow to be 6'6". If I had that height now, I would have had a good shot at playing in the NBA, which was my dream.

But I grew up to be only 6'1", which is an extreme rarity to play in the NBA. However, if I was playing in the NBA, would I have been able to meet my amazing wife, speak all over the world, or write this book you are reading right here, right now?

No!

And guess what? I don't have to shop at the Big and Tall store, so there's another hidden win.

Now it's your turn! Write down your compensation theory (bonus points for doing this activity with your spouse!) and place it next to your work station, office desk, working space, wherever you will see it when you are working to remind you what you thought was a flaw has actually led you to where you are today,

Any situation or circumstance you think is holding you back can actually be the thing that sets you up for something better than you ever expected!

The Mirror of Blame

Have you ever seen the painting of the young beautiful woman and the old hag? I'm sure you probably have, it's an optical illusion. It was created by an anonymous artist in 19th-century Germany to test the mind on perspective.

If you look at it from one perspective, the painting is a beautiful young woman. But if you look at the same painting from a different perspective, you see an old woman.

The eye sees what the eye wants to see.

There is no change in what the retinal image imposed in our eye is actually seeing; however, the visual experience is the variable that changes. The experience, the situation, the circumstances of the painting remain constant. The mental process that transposes the image in the mind, whether it is a positive or negative experience, is what changes.

This is very similar when it comes to blame.

The human brain views *blaming* the same way it views *physical attack*. The prefrontal cortex is at work when you feel you are under a potential threatening physical attack. The same synapses in the prefrontal cortex are at work when you are being blamed and when you are blaming others.

Optical illusions and prefrontal cortex output is all in how we view a situation.

So the question is: What is the one tool that never lies but can be viewed in different ways based on personal perspective?

Answer: A mirror.

Action tool: Choose one mirror in your home. This will be your blaming mirror. Place a sticky note at the top of the mirror you choose (or however you decide to label the mirror) and write "The Blaming Mirror."

Anytime you catch yourself blaming someone else, your situation, a circumstance, or any other external scapegoat, I want you to go to your blaming mirror.

This mirror will serve as an ego check. It's not meant to make you think less of yourself, it's meant to reposition the optical illusion in the mirror.

When you look at yourself in the mirror, I simply want you to point at yourself in the mirror (mentally accepting the blame) and then take that same finger and point to your heart (physically accepting the blame).

By doing this action you have now accepted ownership. And not only that, you have created what is known as *internal psychological ownership*. This is the feeling of possession over a concept, organization, location, or other person. It's why people from Boston are so loyal to their city, or if you are a sports fan of Barcelona soccer, you have a great loyalty to the team. Psychological ownership is associated with a range of positive behaviors including increased loyalty and motivation.

Determine your Mirror of Blame and take ownership today. Trust me, the ownership action you take today will only help you tomorrow!

YOUR ACTION ANIMAL: THE BUTTERFLY EFFECT

How can such a hideous insect transform into a symbol of elegance?

Meet the caterpillar. A fat, constantly hungry eyesore, the caterpillar lurches around throughout the day inch by inch. The caterpillar could look at itself in the mirror and blame its mother for such an ugly face or pudgy body, but it doesn't; it keeps right on moving, slowly but surely.

The caterpillar gets this outlandish idea, "What if I could transform into something beautiful? What if I could fly?"

No, that's way too unrealistic. "Not little old me," thinks the caterpillar.

But instead of blaming its situation, the caterpillar gives it its best shot. The caterpillar releases a hormone call *ecdysone* when it outgrows its skin.

"Now is my chance!" thinks the caterpillar.

But much to its dismay, no transformation occurs. The caterpillar is just a little bit bigger, with even more jiggle in its hips. Again, and again, this process occurs, five times in total until finally the once little caterpillar finds itself hanging upside down in a silky cocoon.

What happens in that cocoon is very interesting and is exactly what is happening to you when you decide to stop blaming your past circumstances.

The caterpillar stops using what is known as the *juvenile* hormone. (How fitting is that?) Now that the caterpillar is no longer a juvenile, it has given itself the permission to grow into the creature it was created to be, a stunning butterfly. The metamorphosis process isn't just a beautiful physical process; it is also a stunning transformation of the mind.

Source: blackdiamond67/Adobe Stock

The butterfly, even though it's the same insect, behaves completely different than the caterpillar. The butterfly soars; it no longer crawls. The butterfly feasts on succulent nectar, no longer larva on the ground. The butterfly is not tied to a tree; it is free to fly anywhere it pleases.

And one of the best parts about the metamorphosis process is that not one single butterfly pattern looks exactly the same as another. Every butterfly is different.

You are different. You are unlike any other person. The things you think hold you back, that you blame for being at a disadvantage, can be transformed into the things that allow you to spread your wings. Don't go through life staying a caterpillar. Your unique, beautiful design is dying to break free and soar. You have grown, you have transformed, you are ready—take action!

Never underestimate the power of dreams and the influence of the human spirit. We are all the same in this notion: the potential for greatness lives within each of us.

—Wilma Rudolph

CHAPTER 5

The Test Believer

MEET ISABEL BRIGGS

For most of her life, Isabel Briggs hid in plain sight, cocooned within the restrictions of what she thought was her destiny. It wasn't that existing in the shadows soothed her more or that she longed to be a social outcast far from the spotlight—not always at least—but it was where she was told she'd find the most peace. And in 1910, young Isabel believed it.

In her daydreams, Isabel lived and spoke in ways only her mind could imagine, but because of the label she'd been given, her body could not. Existing in both the shadows and the spotlight whenever she saw fit was a choice given to others but not Isabel. She was an introvert. And introverts had limitations.

"Isabel, come quickly!" her mother, Katharine, hollered from the foyer. Isabel was 13 years old when she found her mother at the bottom of the stairs flushed with excitement. "I knew it, honey; this confirms it," she boasted, holding up a section of Carl Jung's work *Psychological Types*.

"This article explains exactly why you are an introvert!"

Isabel had heard the word before but on that particular day, it was more than just a word. It was a life sentence. Katharine swore by Carl Jung, the famous Swiss psychiatrist. Deep down she yearned to be more than just a housewife and a mother, and she knew Jung's work was her ticket out. She used every free moment she could spare to collect data and research personality types. The work was exhilarating but daunting. She knew she needed a partner, someone who could help develop her personality tests to reach the masses.

But now, confirming that Isabel was an introvert, Katharine knew her daughter couldn't be that person. It simply wasn't in her making. From now on, she'd refer to Isabel as an example. And Katharine made sure to let her know it.

"Honey, this means you really shouldn't come along to the test groups I conduct anymore. I need someone who is outspoken and draws people in. Sometimes the other children feel uncomfortable as you sit there quietly observing them."

These words cut Isabel like a knife. Pretending to agree, she said a quick "Yes, mother," before withdrawing to her bedroom.

"This is where I belong. I guess I'm better off alone. That's what an introvert does," she softly told herself.

Introvert. The label played over and over in her head. According to the personality test Katharine had created, Isabel exhibited the following traits:

Feels more comfortable focusing on inner thoughts and ideas, rather than what's happening externally. Enjoys spending time with just one or two people. Gains energy through solitude and quiet. Does not excel in group settings.

No matter how many times Isabel took the test, the same result appeared.

Since first learning this, Isabel adhered to her results. She stopped bothering to try growing in the areas it said she wasn't a natural at. Especially when it came to the label of introvert. She longed for friendship and interaction, but she knew it wasn't considered a strength for her.

The fact that Katharine homeschooled Isabel didn't help, either. She rarely got the chance to interact with other children. But what she lacked in communication with others, she made up for with her imagination. Isabel was intensely curious, creating entire worlds in her mind and playing them out through wild adventures in her backyard. Imaginary friends and birds had become Isabel's closest companions.

But when it came time for her to venture out into the real world, that was an issue. The extreme introvert in her would come out, or better said, force her into her shell.

Any time her mother dragged her out into public for errands or holiday events, Isabel would often just sit and observe other people.

"Why does a person act the way they do?" Isabel thought.

She took note of every detailed nuance of someone's personality; however, she never felt confident in sharing her discoveries with her mother.

Years later when she started her first semester at Swarthmore College, Isabel left home but never left her introverted bubble.

Then one day in the school library, interaction found her.

"Excuse me, ma'am, are you reading this?" A tall good-looking, dark-haired man said as he pointed to the book beside Isabel, who was currently nose deep in her own.

Caught off guard by both his question and his magnetic eyes, Isabel only managed to shake her head no.

"Well, don't mind if I do then," he said as he reached for the book.

"What's a pretty lady like you reading about law, anyways?" the man boldly asked as he pulled up a chair to sit next to Isabel.

Isabel shyly looked away, flinching at his abruptness.

"I'm just researching for a book I'm writing," Isabel said without making eye contact.

"You're writing a law book?" The man asked, now having fun teasing the timid Isabel.

"Oh no, not law. I'm writing a novel. I just needed to learn a little background in litigation for my main character," Isabel said, looking at anything but his eyes.

"I see, I see. Well, I'm studying to be a lawyer. Maybe I could teach you a thing or two. How about dinner tonight?" the mystery man asked without hesitation. "Does 7 pm work for you?"

Isabel froze, unable to speak.

"I'm Clarence by the way. Clarence Myers. But most people just call me Chief," the man said extending his hand waiting for Isabel to shake it and accept his dinner date offer.

"So 7 pm works, then?" Chief said with no fear of rejection.

"Yes, 7 pm is fine," she muttered.

That night, Chief managed to bring a side out of Isabel she had never shown before. And, it wasn't long before the two fell in love. The shy, quiet, introverted girl from Michigan and the bold, boisterous, confident farm boy from Iowa.

They were different, very different. But different worked.

Isabel and Chief wed quickly thereafter. Before long, Isabel gave birth to two kids. Chief practiced law while Isabel stayed home to raise the children. As their marriage flourished over the next few years, it occurred to Isabel the common denominator wasn't their similarities, but instead due to their differences in personality that made them a perfect match.

Isabel was an introvert; Chief was an extrovert.

Isabel discovered in herself that by being around Chief, she was able to step out of her introverted shell.

"Could this be true?" Isabel asked Chief one evening. "I'd always thought who you are is *who* you always will be. My mother's personality tests clearly showed I am an introvert."

"But you are not only what your mother's personality test said about you, Isabel. What if there are people just like you who never realize they can actually break the mold?" Chief questioned.

"I want to share what I've discovered with the world, but I can't. I'm not an extrovert like you," she said defeatedly.

"So then you're going to just keep everything you know to yourself? Go on with life even though I can tell you want to do more?" he lovingly questioned.

"I know how to be a housewife. I know how to school the children. This is what introverts are good at," she replied as if reciting off the description of her results from all those years ago.

"Well, what if you ignored what that test said and tried being good at something new?" Chief's words struck a chord.

What was he saying? The test knew her limits. She knew her limits. Or did she?

THE CRUX

Does Isabel decide to shed her introvert handcuffs and step outside of the diagnosis her mother gave her when she was a child? Or does she decide to play it safe and stay in the same spot she is currently in, not taking the risk to step outside her introvert bubble?

***

Your horoscope this month is "You will find great fulfillment and financial prosperity." But wait, it also says you will go through a period of distress and intense dissatisfaction when Venus is in retrograde. But, since you are 7 on the Enneagram with the wing of an 8, you know your enthusiasm and leadership can pull you out of the funk undoubtedly coming your way. Hold on, can you really just enthuse your way out of a Venus retrograde funk? Not if you're an INTP—*the thinker* on the Myers-Briggs Type Indicator. You are highly logical, analytical, and best when processing data, not shouting from the top of a mountain.

By now you are so confused your brain is the one in retrograde! Sound familiar? I know it sounds silly if you read this out loud, but trust me it is far too real. You seek validation for who you are based on a personality test or the way the stars align. But don't beat yourself up for it; it's very common.

The Brain

In a study done by the Pew Research Poll, 29% of US adults believe in their astrology readings. Wow! Nearly one-third base their decisions on the stars. I understand shooting for the stars, but decision-making based on balls of hydrogen and helium? To each their own.

This propensity to accept generic information as your personal truth is called the Barnum effect, also known as Forer effect. It is a psychological phenomenon that explains why individuals believe their personality types are accurate, exact descriptions of their unique personality—no matter how generalized the results might be.

In 1948, psychologist Bertram Forer conducted an experiment on the fallacy of personal validation. Forer's students were given a personality test and told that each questionnaire would be assessed separately and marked with individual feedback by Forer himself. However, instead of providing individualized feedback, Forer gave all participants the same feedback: a paragraph full of very generalized statements. He used sentences like these:

> You tend to be critical of yourself.
>
> Security is one of your major goals in life.
>
> At times you have serious doubts as to whether you have made the right decision.

Once the students received their feedback (not knowing they all received the same information), they rated the accuracy of their profiles on a scale from 0 (poor) to 5 (perfect). The mean accuracy rating was 4.3 out of 5. Thus, almost all the students took Forer's feedback as accurate descriptions of their unique personalities. Forer concluded the results could be attributed to the human tendency to be gullible and an overall desire for *validation*. When the sense of validation arrives, there is no more need to search for a different opinion. You accept it as truth.

For many decades in the past, it was thought the brain was a "nonrenewable" resource, a fixed asset. After conducting studies on the brain's ability to learn new skills, scientists concluded the brain's plasticity was only able to grow during a short window of childhood. They believed the window ended at seven or eight years old.

However, that "critical window for learning" has since been debunked. Scientists at McGill University discovered you can teach an old dog new tricks, and that the plasticity in older adults is actually greater than what was once reported. Now that we know there is no such thing as a *fixed mindset*, we can begin to change the way our brain thinks and even learns.

According to a *Pub-Med* study conducted by psychiatrists Antonio Terracciano and Robert R. McCrae, researchers agree that although personality traits are valuable for analyzing group trends, they are not direct indicators of personal behavior. Human behavior is context-based (the environment in which learners both gain and apply knowledge).

Human beings portray different personalities in different external situations and do not have a fixed personality trait throughout our lifetimes. Contrary to popular belief, your MBTI or Enneagram results can drastically change throughout your lifetime.

Enter oligodendrocytes—the myelinating cells of the central nervous system (CNS). Why is this important to know? Myelination increases the speed by which electrical impulses travel along neuronal processes, allowing the human brain to learn and retain knowledge. You have 86 billion neurons in your brain; each neuron can be connected to up to 10,000 synapses passing signals to each other via as many as 1 trillion synapses.

To break it down to even simpler terms, there is *always* an opportunity to grow, to change, to learn, every single second of every single day. The stars don't dictate your mood, decisions, or actions, and your brain can prove it.

Since the beginning of time, it has been accepted that personality is genetic. However, a landmark study conducted in 2005 by University of Queensland sociology professor Guang Gao discovered that it's not just genetics, but instead a combination of environment and genes that make up the complex human traits. Nature versus future is a false dichotomy. The human being's body and mind react to the outside world.

The point of all this is to understand you are *not* tied to a certain label, stereotype, or way of thinking.

The Heart

We can agree that we have the ability of free will, right? But if our free will is hijacked by a personality test diagnosis, is the free will actually free?

So here is why this can be scary, not just for us as individuals but for society as a whole. Humans thirst for the desire to be a part of "something bigger." That's why we need community. But if our community is dictated by computer-generated data or star alignment, you can see how this might be counter-effective.

"I'm a 3 on the Enneagram; I should only pair up with 9s!"

"I'm an ISTP on the Myers-Briggs; I resonate best with other Crafters!"

Without even realizing it, we create a *confirmation bias*. This means once we have formed a view or identified with a tribe, we embrace information that *only* confirms our view while rejecting any information that would cast doubt on our view. To put it simply, our heart wants us to feel like we belong.

We no longer perceive circumstances objectively. Our world becomes a smorgasbord, picking and choosing pieces of information that fit into our self-created puzzle.

How does this relate to inaction? Very simple: if the results from our personality test tell us to not take action, then we find no need to move forward. For example, if your Myers-Briggs results say you are introverted and you learn introverts are drained by large crowds, you will avoid a career that requires speaking to large crowds.

Or let's say your Enneagram number is a 9, and you read in the description that 9s are peacemakers and want to avoid conflict, then you will surely steer clear of any confrontation.

What should be strictly intel that can be used to help you grow becomes your greatest excuse for being stagnant. Your heart will do anything it can to protect you from failure and hurt, so it only makes sense that it would want you to stick to what you believe is your wheelhouse.

Think about it in your own life. What personality test have you taken that you resonate with? Did you view yourself either in a positive or negative light based on the results? Now, I'm not saying personality tests are bad. A hammer can be the greatest tool when building a house, but it can also be a violent weapon. It's all in how you use it.

The issue with entrusting our decisions to a personality test is this: soon, we unconsciously create our own fences. We become our own self-limiters.

Personality tests essentially create labels. A label is a double-edged sword. On the positive side, it allows people to find a sense of power and belonging with people to whom they can relate. On the flip-side, labels can dictate the expectations you have for yourself and the expectations others have for you, creating stereotypes.

This becomes dangerous because it can result in unrealistic expectations or expecting less from someone capable of more. The label you carry holds a high degree of weight for how you view yourself. But no matter what your personality test *label* says, remember nothing is fixed. Don't allow the results from these tests to be the determining factor behind whether or not your heart lets you take action. Would you ask a magic 8-ball to be your guide for every life decision? I sure hope not.

Use personality tests as a framework to get to know yourself better, making yourself aware of your strengths as well as your weaknesses. Use it as a tool, not a crutch.

What Really Happened to Isabel Briggs?

Isabel tossed and turned in bed that night, unable to shake the thought that maybe her personality typing didn't have to define her.

The next day, she took action and began to research. She stumbled on the Humm-Wadsworth Temperament Scale, a test designed to match people with work aligned to their character. And instead of doing what she normally did, shying away from interaction with others, Isabel took a risk. She decided she was going to seek out a job with Humm-Wadsworth. And the first person she thought to call? Her mother, Katharine.

"What if she just reminds me I have an introvert personality and shoots my idea dead in its tracks?" her mind raced with thoughts like this as she dialed her mother's number.

Much to her surprise, Kathrine was elated. She was taken aback by Isabel's initiative. She encouraged Isabel to go for it, to help allocate people in their right niche within the workforce.

Exuberantly, Isabel went full force into her work with Humm-Wadsworth, but much to her dismay she discovered the indicator was not an effective tool for predicting job performance.

Instead of withdrawing to her bubble in defeat, Katherine reached out to her mother again. And the two decided to tackle the massive venture of creating their own "people-sorting" tool.

It turns out the once-shy, introverted Isabel was anything but the label that had once defined her. She no longer was imprisoned in a life of timidity. In 1943, the world-renowned Myers-Briggs Type Indicator (MBTI) was birthed and the journey to its development began.

Isabel set forth on a mission, knocking on doors, sending out letters, and even giving the test to her son to bring into his high school classes. She didn't let anything stop her; no stone was left unturned nor any door unknocked. The big break for Isabel came with the help of her father, Lyman. Being the director of the Bureau of Standards in

Washington, DC, he had many contacts throughout the academic world. Lyman arranged for the MBTI to be administered to classes in George Washington University Medical School, and the rest was history.

In 1957, the Educational Testing Service signed a contract with Isabel to publish the MBTI, making it the official personality test indicator. Today, MBTI is the most widely used personality indictor throughout the world. An estimated 60 million people have taken MBTI. As of 2020, nearly 1.5 million people take the online test every year and more than 88% of Fortune 500 companies, as well as hundreds of universities, use it in hiring and training.

It's used as a tool in everything from executive development to marital counseling to choosing the best coach for a professional sports team.

Isabel didn't back down. What she proved is that regardless of what a test or anyone labels you to be, *you* and only you get to decide who you actually are.

MBTI, The Enneagram, zodiac signs, DISC Personality, Caliper Profile. None of those really matter. When you are called to take action for a purpose and accomplish meaningful work (as we all are), then nothing, not even a personality test, can stand in your way.

FLIP THE SCRIPT

Now let's imagine what it would look like if Isabel had never taken action.

You wake up on a sunny spring day, ready to embrace the day with a little extra pep in your step. You're feeling great about yourself; life just seems to be swinging your way. Last week you had a major breakthrough. Your boss put you in charge of spearheading the largest acquisition in your company's history and you managed to assemble the dream team of all different personality types. The group contains every strength possible to make this incredible opportunity a sure-fire home run.

As you walk into the company building, whistling your favorite U2 song "Beautiful Day," you stroll past your boss's office and give him a head nod and a wink as if to signify, "Don't worry, I've got this in the bag!'

You stroll into your office and place your notebook on your desk. "Time to get to work," you think. *Success* is waiting for you on a silver platter.

You step out of your office to go rally the troops, the team you spent countless hours vetting to make sure everyone fit perfectly to work together as a team. However, something about the office feels different. Only one of your team members is in the conference room.

"Shannon, where's the rest of the team? Where are Sally, Michael, and John? Tell me they aren't missing today of all days?" you anxiously question your assistant.

"Why would they be here?" Shannon responds with a confused look on her face.

"Because they are a major part of the team we put together for the acquisition project. Why aren't they here?"

"They don't work for our department at all. I'm sorry. You must be mistaken." Shannon replied as if she thought you might be crazy.

You race up the stairs to reach the executive level and head straight to your boss's office.

"Where is my team?" you demand, catching your boss clearly off guard.

"I'm not sure what you're talking about." He responds just as confused as Shannon was.

"The project. You know, for the acquisition? I put together a perfectly matched team of people composed of all different types of personalities," you say as your heart begins to beat faster.

"Mix of personality types? Are you okay? Did you bump your head this morning?" your boss responds, now looking up from his computer with a concerned look on his face.

You are dumbfounded. What just happened?

Here's what happened: Isabel didn't take action. She decided her personality type label of *introvert* defined her and due to her shyness, the dreams and desires to live a life of meaningful work didn't make sense to pursue. An introvert publicly promoting personality tests in a world where personality tests weren't even a thing was far too daunting of a task.

Because of that, people today view personality results as a map of what people can't do, instead of what they can do. Introverts like Isabel aren't hired for energetic, group-oriented companies. Or people who are more energetic and risk-taking aren't hired for more methodical and individualistic companies in industries such as tech and AI. Nobody ever shared with the world that there's a way to match up individual strengths and weaknesses in the work setting to help their workers and companies thrive. And that doing so is actually *necessary* for success. In fact, because Isabel didn't break out of her shell, 70% of the Fortune 500 companies aren't performing as well as they could be. They can't utilize a test like Myers-Briggs to assemble diverse and efficient teams composed of different personality strengths that complement each other. The self-awareness for discovering strengths and weaknesses to optimize teamwork was never created.

***

Why take action if it's not something your personality type can accomplish? Because you aren't defined by the results of a personality test. They can be guides or helpful additions, but in no way, shape, or form do they determine who you are or what you are capable of accomplishing.

Appreciate the tests for what they are. Just remember that what they say you are is not *who* you have to be.

Tools to Overcome the Personality Test Taker

I'm sure you have heard of the *placebo effect*. But I bet you haven't heard of the *nocebo effect?* Both terms stem from the medical world. Placebo is taking a dummy treatment and having a positive result because your mind thought it was taking real medicine. And nocebo is the exact opposite. Imagine that you were told that coffee causes indigestion. You love coffee and drink it every day. Suddenly, you begin to experience symptoms of indigestion because you believe coffee causes it.

The same goes for negative or limiting personality test results. It's great to accept the ones that are positive and boost self-confidence, no harm in that. But if you choose to believe the ones that put you in a box, then you will subconsciously stay in that box. You will begin to feel and exhibit the traits that you don't want to be limited by. All because you believe they are true.

You know *why* you are the test believer; now it's time for me to show you how to conquer this archetype.

Go Retrograde

The word *retrograde* is the most feared word for anyone who reads horoscopes. It basically means "to move backward or move in the opposite direction."

Hmm, interesting. "Move in the opposite direction." There is something to that. Think about it, your life up until this point has been defined by some type of test result.

"Are you really the way you are because you were born in a certain month of the year?" The late Trevor Mowad told a story about one of the most famous magazine editors of all time who struggled throughout high school. He was unable to keep up with the other kids, fell behind in every class, and nearly flunked out, all while being raised by a single mother.

The time came to take the SAT, the standard testing to determine if the student was smart enough to get into college. The boy didn't expect much from the test, and his mother had all but given up hope on her son. But much to both of their surprise, the boy achieved a genius score: 1480!

The boy became so motivated by his newfound brilliance, he decided to attend junior college directly out of high school where he earned good enough grades to attend Wichita State the following year. But why stop there? He took a chance by applying to attend an Ivy League school and was accepted. He graduated and eventually went on to be one of the most successful and prominent magazine editors of all time.

Years later, the successful editor received a letter from the SAT testing service. The letter stated that the year he took the SAT, he was one of thirteen people to have been given an *incorrect* test score. His actual score was only 740, a result that would never be mentioned in the same sentence as the word *genius*.

The test result was defining. Luckily for him, he got the *wrong* defining result. Had this boy seen the score of 740 when he was in high school, he would have never believed he could achieve anything great.

Have you limited yourself to a certain personality type based on a test you took or an assessment from a professional? Do you see the negative score on your sleep tracking app and believe you should "take it easy today" because it recommended you do so? Does a high school test score, which barely has any relevance to real-world experience, determine your level of intelligence for the rest of your life?

The answer to all of these is no. Go retrograde. Go against the grain. You determine the person you want to become, not a personality test.

Take this action today: Read the following phrases in the Go Retrograde Test and place a checkmark next to each one that applies to you.

Go Retrograde Test

- Values integrity; wants to be balanced
- Is ambitious and goal-oriented
- Can come up with creative ideas that wouldn't occur to most people
- Embodies the gifts of charisma and confidence
- Values feeling loved
- Playful sense of humor, very entertaining
- Cares deeply about integrity
- Values feeling valuable and worthwhile
- Compassionate and nonjudgmental, always willing to hear another person's story

- Has a passion and charisma that inspires others
- Values having significance (to create an identity)
- Has easygoing exteriors with a rich, vibrant inner life
- Is respected for reliability and practicality
- Values being capable and competent
- Hardworking and devoted
- Values honesty, dedication, and dignity
- Believes in the power of hospitality and good manners
- Enjoys lending a hand and sharing experiences
- Unassuming and humble
- Values having security and support
- Always has an impact on immediate surroundings
- Generous with time and energy
- Values satisfaction and contentment—needs fulfilled
- Loves to be number one
- Enjoys relaxing in serene, idyllic environments
- Spontaneous, playful, and adorably erratic
- Highly intuitive
- Values protection
- Passionate and loyal
- Isn't afraid to improve skills through diligent and consistent practice
- Strives to create equilibrium in all areas of life
- Has powerful wisdom through both the physical and mental realms
- Enjoys an exciting adventure

- Values inner stability, peace of mind
- Is dedicated and able to persevere
- Committed to making the world a better place
- Intuitive and empathetic to others

Now count up all of your checkmarks.

Did a lot of these apply to you? Probably so. Ironically the test you just took was strengths from all 9 Enneagram Types, all 16 Myers-Briggs personalities, and all 12 zodiac signs. Is it possible to match various characteristics from every single type of personality test?

Yeah, it is.

So before you go labeling yourself an Aquarius, Peacemaker, or INFJ (Advocate), pump the breaks. There is no personality test of any kind that can define who you are.

On a piece of paper, create your own personality type. Write "The _____ (fill in the blank with your name) Retrograde." Then below, list every single personality trait you want to possess. It can be anything and be as many characteristics as you want. From now on, *you*, and only you, define who you are and who you are going to be.

Embrace the *retrograde* of your life.

PTA Test

The PTA test is the only self-rating test you truly need. It has nothing to do with typology, and it will never be limiting. It is a test focused solely on your own self-awareness, and it encourages growth. All it requires is for you to assess three personal aspects:

- Presence
- Trust
- Acceptance

Action for the day: At the end of *every* day, do this quick and simple self-analysis test. *(Credit to mental skills guru Graham Betchart for this tool.)* You can write it in your journal every evening, you can share it with your spouse or loved ones, or you can take note internally. Regardless, make a heavy emphasis to implement the PTA tool into your daily routine. You can't measure what you don't track.

Presence: How present were you?

Ask yourself these questions: How present were you throughout the day? In the current moment, in your relationships, with your family and friends, at your job—how present were you? Did you find yourself often thinking about other things, daydreaming, or hearing what someone said but not actually listening to their words?

Rate yourself on a scale of 1–100 (1: not present; 100: fully present)

Trust: Do you trust the process of your day-to-day?

Ask yourself these questions: Do you believe that where you are right now, in this very moment, is exactly where God wants you to be? Do you trust your daily habits? Do you trust those whom you surround yourself with? Do you trust yourself? Do you trust there is a bright future ahead of you without doubt?

Rate yourself on a scale of 1–100 (1: not trusting; 100: full trusting)

Acceptance: Are you able to accept the things you can't control and control the things you can?

Ask yourself these questions: Did you at any point in the day wonder, "why me"? Do you accept who you are? Do you accept your past? Do you accept that no matter what happens, you will make it through and become better because of it?

Rate yourself on a scale of 1–100 (1: not accepting; 100: fully accepting

Your Action Animal: The Chameleon

When you think about the chameleon, the first thought that probably comes to mind is a shapeshifter: an animal that changes its appearance to fit into the environment.

But that's not the main reason chameleons change colors. They're less concerned with their outside surroundings (i.e., external circumstances in your life) and more concerned about regulating their internal body temperature (i.e., your internal self-belief).

Source: Dmitry/Adobe Stock

Chameleons have two layers of what are called *iridophores*. These iridophores have pigments and nanocrystals within that reflect the lights of different wavelengths. This enables the chameleon to change its color by exciting or relaxing its skin, which changes the density of the upper layer of iridophores.

When a chameleon is in a relaxed state, the nanocrystals in the skin are closer to each other, creating shorter wavelengths and a bluer tone. When a chameleon is excited, the distance between nanocrystals increases, creating longer wavelengths and reflecting warmer colors such as red, orange, and yellow.

Think about it: the chameleon isn't defined by how it was born, and the chameleon doesn't change because it is worried about fitting a certain mold.

The two main reasons chameleons change their color are to regulate body temperature and to communicate. Males often change color to attract a mate. You want to find a significant other? Quit dressing like the Aquarius description of your monthly horoscope or the shy INFJ score on your Myers-Briggs test.

Embrace the chameleon within you and decide who *you* want to be. Have you ever been in an awkward situation where you wanted to change the temperature of the room? Yeah, we all have. The chameleon within you gives you the ability to shift your iridophores, allowing *you* and only you to have ownership over your feelings, not someone else.

"You psychologists focus on what is wrong with people; I want to focus on what is right and what could be right."

—Isabel Briggs

CHAPTER 6

The Perfectionist

MEET WARD PIGGY LAMBERT

Ward Piggy Lambert liked control. Even as a teenager, he had a rigid need for the best and only the best. If things were going to run smoothly, and they damn well better, Piggy had a rock-solid, one-man plan to make sure it happened. Everyone who knew him knew it was Piggy's way or the highway, a deep-seated trait that didn't earn him many fans on the basketball court.

"Piggy, pass the ball for goodness' sake! You've been dribbling it all game," scolded one of his teammates during the time-out huddle. Truth is, Ward's teammate was right. Ward was a bona fide ball hog, hence the nickname *Piggy*.

"You weren't open," contended Piggy. "Someone has to lead this team, and we sure as heck know it's not you."

As the point guard and leading scorer on the Wabash University basketball team, Piggy was a control freak and a perfectionist; he always wanted to have the ball in his hands, control the tempo of the game, and take the important shots. The formula didn't always translate to team wins.

Most teammates didn't enjoy playing on the same team as Piggy because of his tendency to boss them around and point out their flaws. "You know, you'd make a much better coach, Piggy," one of his teammates chimed in sarcastically after another loss.

Piggy didn't know how to take that comment. Did he mean it, or was it a shot at his need for control and lack of *actual* basketball talent?

Piggy graduated from Wabash University in 1911, after a less-than-impressive college basketball career. Without any real plans for after college, he returned home to his family in Crawfordsville, Indiana.

"It's time to get a job now, Piggy," his mother declared at dinner one night. "They're hiring down at the local factory. That new assembly line of motor vehicles just opened in town. The Henry Ford automobile. Good wages, I hear."

But a factory job held no appeal for Piggy, All he had ever known was basketball. "Ma, I'm going to be a basketball coach. I was made for this sport." Piggy said, dodging any talk of the auto factory.

"Okay, son, but just know that playing and coaching are two very different things," his mother quickly chimed back. Shrugging off her words, Piggy decided to apply for the head high school coaching job in the nearby town of Lebanon, Indiana.

And sure enough, he got the job.

But before Piggy could celebrate, the phone rang. It was Ralph Jones, the coach he played for at Wabash University. Coach Jones was leaving Wabash to coach for Purdue University, which was only 35 miles down the road from Lebanon. He wanted to have a word before Piggy began his coaching career.

"Piggy, coaching isn't all about being in control. You can't control every player on the team, nor can you control every situation on the floor. Being a great coach isn't about controlling, it's about leading."

"Yeah, leading, that's what I'm going to do," said Piggy without hesitation, not fully grasping the point Coach Jones was trying to make.

"Okay, Piggy, then you're going to need this," Coach Jones reached into his desk and pulled out a whistle. "But remember: with this whistle comes great responsibility."

"I know, Coach, I know. You can trust me," he assured his former coach, unaware of the challenges to come.

The night of the first high school game in Lebanon, the stands were jam-packed. The excitement in the air was tangible. Piggy breathed it in. This is what he lived for; this is what he was made to do.

Piggy was in his office going over his game plan for the umpteenth time when the Lebanon team captain marched in.

"Coach, I just wanted to let you know that you can count on me. I'll help us win this game tonight," he stated.

"Oh it's okay, son, I've got this. I've got the plan. You just execute the plan, and we'll be just fine."

What the players on the Lebanon High School team didn't know is that Piggy suffered from a severe case of *perfectionism*. If he didn't feel like he was in control of every situation, then Piggy's life spun out of control.

From the moment the ball was tipped to start the game, Piggy paced up and down the sidelines barking orders at his players. A barrage of nonstop verbal instructions flooded the court as if the players were robots and couldn't think for themselves.

Lebanon fell behind quickly, and the margin of deficit continued to grow larger and larger as the game continued. Piggy could feel himself spinning out, losing all control. Then, late in the second half as the game was all but out of reach, Piggy collapsed to the ground. The game abruptly came to a stop and the audience froze as he lay gasping for air.

"Are you okay, Coach?" asked one of his Lebanon players as they quickly surrounded Piggy with shock and fear.

"*Umnnhh*" was all Piggy could muster as he was lifted onto a stretcher and rushed to the emergency room.

Piggy was examined for injuries and brain aneurysms. All tests thankfully came back negative. However, the doctors told him he had suffered a severe panic attack. The perfectionist in him had gotten the best of him.

"Piggy, you doing all right?" said a familiar voice standing over his hospital bed. It was Coach Jones.

"Yeah, Coach, I'm fine." Piggy replied in a self-defeated voice.

"Remember what I told you when you were in my office? Control and leading are two very different things. You don't need to control every situation in the game; you need to empower your players to play to the best of their abilities. That's what coaching is about—leadership and empowerment, not control," Coach Jones reminded Piggy, almost as if he was an angel sent to deliver that message.

Those words were exactly what Piggy needed to hear.

He returned to work and let go of the reins he had once gripped so tightly. He went on to coach Lebanon High School for the next three seasons, amassing a record of 69–18, including a trip to the state tournament.

After the third season, Piggy received a call from a familiar voice.

"Piggy, I've decided to retire from Purdue. I'm stepping down, and I wanted to know if you would be interested in taking over the team," Coach Jones asked from the other line. "But under one condition, though, Piggy: you remember what I told you that night after the first game you coached? Leadership and control are two very different things. Have you learned that lesson?"

"Oh, I know, Coach. Trust me I've learned my lesson and then some," Piggy said with a smile the size of the state of Indiana.

Flash forward to 1932 and Piggy was still the coach for the Boilermakers. He had tasted success and setbacks over the last 15 years; he even had to miss a year of coaching to serve in the US Army in World War I. The perfectionist in Piggy still reared its ugly head at times. In his time as coach, it became an *expectation* to win at Purdue. Anything less was deemed a failure. And who would everyone blame if they lost? The coach. Piggy knew that. His need for ultimate control rose to the surface and begged to break through.

There was a senior point guard, John, whom Piggy butted heads with multiple times over the previous few years. The question wasn't whether or not he was talented—he was already an All-American—the question was whether he was good enough to be the leader Piggy needed him to be to ensure a victorious season. This year would be Purdue's best chance to win the national championship. So for Piggy, it was now or never.

During an early season practice, John shouted over Piggy's voice from the sidelines, hollering "Coach, I've got this! Guys, let's run play 2."

"John Wooden, get your butt on the baseline right this moment. You're running sprints for the rest of practice." John paused mid-scrimmage, holding the ball on his hip as he turned slowly to address Piggy with a confused look on his face.

"Coach, with all due respect, I'm just doing my job," John calmly responded as if he wasn't fazed by the imposing threat from Piggy.

"I said on the baseline, dammit," Piggy was not about to back down.

John placed the ball directly on the baseline and stormed out of the gym and into the locker room. He'd heard enough. Why would he stay at a school that didn't appreciate the talented leader he was?

THE CRUX

Will Piggy give control of the team to John Wooden and allow him to lead Purdue to a national championship? Or will he let his need for control and perfectionism get the best of him?

***

Ready. Aim. Aim. Aim some more, keep aiming. Go back and make adjustments. It's not ready to show to the world. What if people were to see your work right now?! Oh, the horror! Think of what they would say about you. You, the one who always gets it right, the one who always has it perfect. You're not ready; maybe this was a bad idea to begin with. Maybe it's better if you don't take the chance. No one has to know, only you and your conscience. You'll be okay, you'll get over it. Far better than being humiliated in public by putting out something less than perfection. Your unblemished streak will live on.

Or will it?

Has your mind engaged on a similar rollercoaster of perfection-ism? Have you had a great idea for a business but kept going back to the business plan to *tinker*? Have you written 20 chapters of your book but can't ever fathom actually releasing it to the world? Are you afraid to share your vulnerable side with your friends because you fear they will discover the real you? Keep it buttoned up, you tell yourself, no one has to know.

Let me introduce to you Maxwell Johnston, the CEO and founder of JustRight, and his fascinating story. Max had a dream to leave his corporate job and start his own company. But Max had never done anything remotely risky. He had always executed his precisely crafted plan with perfection. He graduated valedictorian of his high school class, attended an ivy league college on a full academic scholarship, graduated with honors, and transitioned right into a high-paying cor-porate job. He always did everything by the book and everything that was asked of him.

However, even though he succeeded at these things, deep down he longed for more. He dreamt of doing something outside the box, something riskier and outside of his comfort zone. Whenever Max had downtime at his corporate job, he would pour his energy into his dream business: JustRight. He put in hours before work, after work, even on the weekends; he invested extra time to ensure that one day he would be able to leave the office life behind and work only for himself.

Finally, the time came; Max was ready to launch JustRight. He set the launch date and his closest friends and family were going to gather together at a lunch party in celebration. The release of his new com-pany was going to change not only his life but the lives of so many other people. But something was off; Max got a last-minute case of cold feet. So he postponed the launch and went back to the drawing board to *tinker*. He had to get it right. This was his one and only chance; he couldn't swing and miss on the launch, or he might be stuck in his corporate job for the rest of his life!

Max went back to his routine: before work, after work, on the weekends, pouring time into making sure JustRight was perfect for launch. After several weeks of this, Max felt ready. He called his family and closest friends and let them know it was time. Everyone was excited for Max; this was going to be life-changing!

However, the day before the launch Max called it off *again*. There was a small piece Max just felt he was missing, and without this piece, the business would never succeed. He couldn't launch like this. Back to the drawing board, back to *tinkering*.

If you're wondering how the story ends, I think you are catching on. Maxwell Johnston never launched JustRight. He never could get it "just right." So instead of launching and learning along the way, Max kept it on the inside, close to his chest. The perfectionist in him won out. And the world remained unchanged.

Max is a fictional character, but his story is all too real. Can you feel it in your life? When was the last time you wanted to take action on a dream, start a new business, or learn a new instrument, but you were paralyzed by the weapon of mass destruction: *perfectionism*?

The Brain

According to Dr. Thomas Curran and Dr. Andrew Hill, there are three types of perfectionism:

- Self-oriented (an irrational desire to be perfect)
- Socially prescribed (perceiving excessive expectations from others)
- Other-oriented (placing unrealistic standards on others)

In their study, Curran and Hill analyzed the data of 41,641 US, British, and Canadian students between 1980 and 2016. Their findings concluded that recent generations recorded a significantly higher incidence of the three forms of perfectionism than did their predecessors in previous generations. From 1989 to 2016, the self-oriented perfectionism score increased by 10%, socially prescribed increased by 33%, and other-oriented increased by 16%.

Why is this?

Simple, the rise of meritocracy. There is more pressure than ever to perform. Earning a college degree was once a celebrated anomaly but has now become a baseline expectation. The expectations society has created are at an all-time high. It's no wonder mental health issues, depression, and suicide rates are also at an all-time high.

The pressure to project an inauthentic version of yourself, your goals, your life, has created these unrealistic expectations. Take Instagram, for example. I bet if you went on there right now, you'd be hard-pressed to find a post where someone exposes all the failures, mishaps, and heartbreaks behind a recent success. We log on and scroll through a barrage of polished images that may leave you feeling dissatisfied and inadequate. Everywhere you look someone's living in your dream house, vacationing on your dream island, eating your dream meal, reaping the benefits of everything you aspire to achieve. The thing is, it's only a tiny slice of the picture. Barely even a glimpse. Slapping a pretty filter on the fruits of your labor is a surefire way to garner some serious likes. Showing the actual labor, well, as helpful as those snapshots might be, they rarely make it off the camera roll.

For those who are at a place in their career that you aspire to achieve, you don't get to see every single detail of their journey and the moments of imperfection that they had. For those who have the dream spouse and relationship you long for, they don't have a profile decorated with evidence of all the bad dates and lonely nights they endured before they met their spouse. They don't share the imperfections in their relationship that you envy as being flawless. You can see it in magazine covers, commercials, social media, and even something that should be as simple as a Yelp or Google review. Businesses do everything they can to incentivize a five-star review online because appearing perfect is the only way society deems it worthy of our business. So it's no wonder that subconsciously you strive to appear perfect and feel held back from doing anything that might be labeled as less than.

But, if you are striving to be flawless before taking action, stop. It will never work. You will drive yourself nuts trying to be perfect. Literally, no human being to walk this planet other than Jesus has lived a perfect life. So what makes you think you are going to? Not only is it impossible, it's also not required. Hopefully, that alleviates some pressure.

Let's look at how perfectionism works at a neurobiological level in the brain. The area of the brain in charge of *perfectionism* (error-processing) is the anterior cingulate cortex (ACC). The ACC is directly correlated with emotion assessment and emotion-related learning. When perfectionists commit an error (the deadly sin of a perfectionist), the ACC kicks into overdrive assessing the emotion and sending the person into a flight state.

In a study done by Jutta Stahl and researchers at Cologne University, they found participants with external judgment–based perfectionism dealt with error-processing much less effectively than those with internal judgment–based perfectionism. They concluded that the perfectionism we feel is not as much our own standards and expectations weighing us down, but instead the pressure from the outside world screaming at us that we have to be perfect.

Understanding how the brain deals with perfectionism can help you understand why this is such a struggle in your life. You tell yourself the lie that you want to have everything perfect because "it is your own standards." But that's not the truth. The loneliness you feel, the anxiety, the stress, that doesn't come from "well, it's just the way I was wired." No, that comes from "I have to be perfect because others expect it of me."

You are type A; you are a high achiever, I get that. But you won't ever get anything done if you never take action or put anything out in the world because you are in fear of it not being *perfect*.

The most common mental distortion among perfectionists is "all-or-nothing thinking." Everything is either black or white; there are no shades of gray.

> You didn't get an A on your exam: you are a failure.
>
> You didn't get the most sales within the company this month: you should just give up.
>
> Your kid didn't win the soccer game: what a shame to the family name.

Life is lived in the gray areas. It is very rare that anything is black or white.

People who are perfectionists typically believe that nothing they do is worthwhile unless it is flawless. They aren't able to enjoy the learning process, feel a sense of accomplishment after a hard day's work, or acknowledge any visible growth because they are too focused on producing a perfect result. They set their personal bar of success at the same level as other successful people, failing to recognize that the other successful people failed many times along their journey to success.

The fear of failure keeps a perfectionist from ever trying. "Why try if I am going to inevitably fail?" We've heard it a million times: the best way to learn and grow is through failing. So how will you ever grow if you never experience the benefit of failing?

The Heart

Perfectionism is often celebrated in society. The one who doesn't ever settle for "less than" is the one who is held in high regard. But once our heart make its mission to only celebrate the good and never laugh at ourselves or celebrate our bloopers, failures, and mishaps, it causes what is known as *overgeneralization.*

Perfectionists tend to also overgeneralize every situation, creating a feeling of distortion in which the individual views a single event as an invariable rule.

> The basketball player who misses one free throw thinks "My shot is broken; I can never make a free throw." He feels defeated and incapable of doing what he loves. A feeling of distortion.

> The dancer who misses a step during her team's routine thinks "I have two left feet; I always mess up." She feels unworthy of being on stage. Another feeling of distortion.

Overgeneralizing gives you a very small margin of error, one that is far outside the healthy limits and places immense stress on your heart.

Do you find yourself thinking and feeling these same things? Are there any gray areas in your life? If you messed up once, does that mean you will always mess up?

So am I saying you should just throw anything out into the world even if it's not ready yet?' No. That's definitely not what I am saying. But an obsessive drive for flawlessness will lead to diminishing returns.

How does one develop *perfectionism?* Are you born with it? I've got good and bad news for you. While there can be a genetic component to perfectionism, there is no strong evidence to show that people are born with high levels of it. Unfortunately, the bad news is that environmental factors play a significant role in the development of perfectionism. Most perfectionism is learned, and one of the key time frames this occurs is during interactions with your parents in childhood. If your parents only rewarded you for an outstanding performance and punished you for anything less, you became conditioned to the praise response. Anything less would trigger a tongue-lashing pain that encompasses your heart. And if getting that praise meant pursuing the road of perfection, your heart will still automatically steer you in that direction.

The difficult part is that perfectionism isn't a switch you can turn on and off; it becomes ingrained in you. Once you have developed a perfectionist mindset, it is nearly impossible to reverse your way of thinking. I say "nearly" because I am going to show you exactly how you can break the chains of perfectionism and take action toward your dreams even if you don't have every *t* crossed or every *i* dotted.

WHAT ACTUALLY HAPPENED TO PIGGY LAMBERT?

Piggy's eyes tracked Wooden as he disappeared into the locker room. He had blatantly ignored Piggy's directive, as though immune to his control. Teammates murmured from the sidelines, but all Piggy could hear was the sound of his own blood pounding through his veins.

Time seemed to stand still, frozen by on-court tension.

A calm voice arose in the back of Piggy's mind, cooling his resentment. They were the words of Coach Jones, "Being a great coach isn't about controlling, it's about leading."

He needed to give Wooden the necessary space to lead. And from that moment on, he did, allowing John to call his own plays as the point guard of the team.

Piggy Lambert and Purdue University finished that 1932 season with a 17–1 record, retroactively being named the national champions by the Helms Athletic Foundation and the Premo-Porretta Power Poll (a committee appointed in 1939 to review decades of past seasons and decide who the best teams in college basketball were for every year; prior to this there were no rankings). The 1932 season was remarkable because Piggy gave control to his point guard, John Wooden.

Piggy desired control. But his greatest asset was the self-control that allowed him to hand over the reins to John. He learned he could not and did not need to be in control all of the time.

Piggy would go on to coach 16 All-American players, and Purdue even changed the name of their home arena from Purdue Fieldhouse to Lambert Fieldhouse in honor of Piggy. On top of that, his leadership skills were so highly regarded, that Purdue asked him to simultaneously coach the baseball team. The school eventually named their baseball field after him: Lambert Field.

But the greatest impact Piggy left was the legacy of leadership he taught the fiery senior point guard John Wooden, who became arguably the greatest coach of all time in *any* sport. John set the standard of excellence, a bar that he raised so high, it will likely never be touched again.

The legacy of John Wooden, however, might have never been possible if, at that practice in 1932, Coach Lambert hadn't taken action. Piggy's decision to relinquish his need for *perfectionism* opened up the space for John Wooden to flourish; ultimately Piggy's choice to take action that day changed the world forever.

"Success is never final, failure is never fatal, and it's courage that counts."

—John Wooden

FLIP THE SCRIPT

Now let's imagine what it would look like if Piggy Lambert didn't take action and instead hogged control throughout his entire coaching career.

It's game day! Your favorite college basketball team is playing for the national championship. "Will this finally be the year?" You think out loud, unable to hold it in.

You fill your favorite mug—the one with your team logo on it, of course—with coffee and hop in your car and drive to work, listening to the local broadcast and "expert analysis" predictions on the outcome of the game while drumming your thumbs on top of the steering wheel and bobbing your head back and forth.

But as one of the analysts begins to talk negatively about your team, you immediately cut the audio. "How dare he!" you think. "This joker never played basketball yet he has the audacity to talk trash on my team?"

So you decide to listen to your favorite self-development podcast in hopes of shifting your negative emotions into positive ones. You stop at a red light, and scroll through the potential podcasts to tune into, but none of the personal development ones are showing up.

"What the heck is going on?" you wonder. It must just be that your podcast app is bugging out and you need to restart your phone. But that doesn't work, either.

Confused, but not wanting to turn back on the radio and hear the knucklehead who was lambasting your team, you decide to pick up where you left off in the audiobook you have been listening to: "Finding the Better YOU Inside of You." But that isn't coming up, either.

"Piece of junk phone," you mutter as you toss it into the passenger seat as the light turns green. Is there some kind of software bug infesting only the personal development podcasts in your phone? Oh, well, you will be at the office soon and be able to focus on getting your work completed and then back home to watch the game.

It's tough to not be in a positive state of mind at your office with all the inspirational quotes that cover the walls. You look forward to seeing them as you enter. But as you walk through the front doors, instantly something is off. "Why are the walls so barren?" you think. "Where did Wooden's pyramid of success poster go?" Something is wrong. Very wrong.

As you continue down the hallway, no one even bothers to lift their head to give you a friendly nod or smile. "Did someone get fired?" you think to yourself as you enter your office, your safe space of positivity.

But your wall is bare—your favorite inspirational pictures with quotes are gone—and nothing more than the pictures of you and your family lay scattered on your desk. "Was the office robbed?" You open the door and yell, "What is going on here?!"

Here is what is going on here: Ward Piggy Lambert never gave up the reins of control to John Wooden. Wooden never went on to be the coach and leader he was or become a pioneer in the personal development space. And your beloved team—the one you thought would battle for the national championship that evening—wasn't even worth staying up to watch.

Piggy's release of perfectionism in 1932 changed the trajectory of leadership and coaching as we know it.

What are you holding on to today that you need to let go of? What do you need to just press "go" on and get out there in the world? Is your desire for control and your need to have every aspect of everything you do be "perfect" suffocating not only you but also the others around you?

Perfectionism is a roadblock to progress. You will never be perfect. You will never have it all together. You will never be fully in control. No one is perfect, or ever will be. Free yourself from the lie that you must have it all together. Dance in public with your two left feet.

TOOLS TO OVERCOME THE PERFECTIONIST

1. If it's raining, then the streets are wet.

2. The streets are wet.

3. Therefore, it's raining.

Makes sense, right? This is what is known as *affirming the consequent*. But think about it, the streets could actually be wet because a fire hydrant blew a casquet and drenched the entire street. Instead, this rigidity of thinking is exactly what happens when you allow perfection-ism to be your guide.

1. If you get the job, you had the pitch and presentation perfected.

2. You had the pitch and presentation perfected.

3. Therefore, you got the job.

But it's not true. As you can see, affirming the consequent can become dangerous as you will begin to think:

- If x, then y.

- Not x.

- Therefore, not y.

Nothing in life functions in black-and-white formulas. Everything is gray. And that's what I want you to discover. Perfectionism is black and white; there is no room for gray. Perfectionism is a fallacy.

You know *why* you are the perfectionist; now it's time for me to show you how to conquer this archetype.

The 90% Rule

"Give it your all! Go 100% 100% of the time!" How many times have you heard that? Or if you are like me, you are the person who hates when someone says, "Give it 110%!" How is that even possible? That's like a high school student who graduates with 4.5 on a 4.0 scale. What? Where do we draw the line?

The actual key to reaching the highest state of your success *flow* is not at 100% but instead at 90%. Sounds contradictory, right? It should.

Take the fitness world, for example. To achieve the best heart health, mitochondrial density, and VO2 max (oxygen capacity), the sweet spot to train in is what is called Zone 2. If you push to 100% output, you will overdo your body and your mind and you will quickly burn out. The short-term benefits might show in the interim, but the long-term determinants will ultimately erode your body and mind.

The same thing holds true when it comes to all aspects of life. If you are dating a girl and you answer every text just seconds after she texts you, if you are always free whenever it works for her schedule, if you get her flowers on every date, and if you tell her how much you love her too early on, you will undoubtedly (I hope for her sake) scare her away.

If you are trying to get a promotion in your sales business and you respond to every email seconds after you hear the inbox notification, if you constantly pitch your product during every phone call with prospective clients, if you talk only about what you can provide for the client, you will turn the client off regardless of whether the product you are selling is good or not.

A study led by Harry Ries at Rochester University concluded that "playing hard to get" does in fact work. His coauthor in the study, Gurit Birnbaum, states, "Playing hard to get makes you seem as if you are in more demand."

100% will not get you to 100% of where you want to be.

Effort that looks *effortless* will. Embrace the 90% rule.

Action step for the day: What is the most challenging thing on your schedule for today or this week? Take a minute to ask yourself that question. Now, what if you viewed that "challenging thing" as a challenge you had already conquered. Do you think you would have more peace about it? Do you think you would feel more confident in it? I would imagine so. Because you have already accomplished it.

This is a tactic I teach to NBA players who are struggling with shooting free throws (free shots when no one is defending them from the same distance on the court every time). The pressure they place on themselves leads them to *trying* too hard to make the shot and causes them to actually *miss* the shot at a higher percentage. The same goes for short puts in golf.

Write on a piece of paper: "I've Already Won the Game." Place this paper near your bedstand or bonus points for taping it to the ceiling directly above your bed (first thing your eyes will see every morning when you wake up!).

You have already won the game. Take a deep breath in; you no longer have to *press* 100% of the time. How freeing is that? *Now* you can operate in your flow state.

Failure Stats

When was the last time a sports team of any level tracked *failure stats* in the box score? I'm taking wild a guess here, but I would lean toward *never*. We all can agree that failure will occur, right? So, if failure is going to happen, why don't we build our failures into our plans and celebrate them? Instead of trying to put as much cover-up on blemishes that in actuality make us better.

Let's forget that we are talking about failure for a second. If I were to ask you, "Do you want your brain to grow?" I'm guessing your answer, without hesitation, would be a big fat yes!

And what if I were to tell you one of the most effective ways for your brain to grow is through the release of cortisol in your brain? The brain releases the hormone cortisol when the body is stressed (i.e., failure is an extreme stressor on the body). On the outside, failure can seem like the end of the world as we know it. But on the inside, it is hidden growth.

A 2015 study done at the University of Southern California concluded that the brain learns in either one of two ways: through avoidance learning or reward-based learning. Scientists found that the optimal way for the brain to learn is through failure when it is tied to reward-based learning. When the subject was allowed and encouraged to "learn from their mistakes," the amount of growth in the brain was higher than for those of avoidance learning or even success-driven, reward-based learning.

When given the opportunity and a safe space to fail, we grow. So, it only makes sense to build these *failures (growth) stats* into your year!

Action step for today: Write down all of the big flops and failures you have had this year. Here are some of mine:

- Drove to the wrong coffee spot for an important meeting I had with the CEO of a company to potentially lock down a big keynote speech. Epic fail.

- Didn't proofread a text I sent to a friend; they interpreted it the wrong way, and it took a month of trying to mend the relationship.

- Reached out to a contact (an agent) to ask if I could work with their player (multi-million-dollar star). I didn't ask how the agent was doing or even care to ask what I could do to help the agent. I went straight for the ask because of what I wanted. Failure. Relationship strained.

That is three already for me! And trust me, there are many more on that list. Now the next part is the real perfectionist-defeating key: write down *future* failures that you will build into the upcoming months ahead. I'll go first:

- I will sign up for five minutes at a standup comedy club, and (more than likely) fall flat on my face and get booed off the stage.

- I will take a shot at a major consulting deal with a company, knowing they will likely laugh at my offer and turn me down. (But who knows, it could work!)

- I will take a salsa dancing class with my wife even though I have zero rhythm or flow and will absolutely suck at it.

I will fail at all three of these *future* endeavors. And by failing, I know I will grow. I don't have to be perfect, and I will never be perfect. And I'm perfectly okay with not being perfect.

YOUR ACTION ANIMAL: THE SQUIRREL

Perfectionism is like a squirrel trying to find the perfect nut. If only it existed. A squirrel's entire existence revolves around finding and storing food. Now, this might sound like an *obsession*, but when you realize squirrels often forget where they buried their food, you might chuckle. Here is this animal fighting daily for survival, spending all its waking hours searching for food, and yet it often forgets where it's buried. It's God's way of saying, "Don't take yourself so seriously." You don't have to be perfect. Even if you put your life's work into something, you are never going to be perfect, just like the squirrel.

Have you ever watched a squirrel zig and zag through the branches of a tree? It's incredible. They are flexible and nimble acrobats. As they dart from one limb to the next, they don't have the luxury of time to scope out the situation ahead and make sure everything is in the correct order. No, not even close. Squirrels will often miss a branch and fall, barreling down to the ground. But if you have seen a squirrel do this before, it looks more like a planned acrobatic routine than it does a misstep leading to a fall.

Source: henk bogaard/Adobe Stock

There's no doubt that you will trip and stumble, but just like the squirrel, you can have confidence knowing that your fall doesn't have to end with a thud. It can be an acrobatic triple-double, with a landing at the bottom that you stick.

You might be thinking, "But what happens if I hit all the branches on the way down and land face-first 'splat' on the ground?" Don't worry, unlike other mammals, the squirrel can defy terminal velocity (the constant force [speed] on a falling object). If other mammals fall from great heights, they fall to their demise. But not the squirrel. And not you.

You don't have to be perfect. You will lose a majority of the nuts you bury anyways. Take a breath and laugh at yourself. And if you fall? All the better, because just like the acrobatic squirrel, you will fall, you will survive, and no matter how hard the landing is at the bottom, you will get right back out there and keep climbing.

Embrace your action animal, the squirrel, and start taking the chance even before you have it all together. Take the leap!

"The team that makes the most mistakes usually wins."
—Ward Piggy Lambert

CHAPTER 7

The Scarciest

MEET JAMES HARRISON

The ambulance sirens screamed to a halt outside the emergency room of the bustling Australian hospital. Young James Harrison, all of 14 years old, laid on the stretcher, with an eerie calm as if he sensed his premature life would soon come to an end.

James needed major chest surgery, and the odds of surviving were a coin flip. "Mum," James struggled to mutter. "Am I going to be okay?"

"Yes, of course, dear," his mother reassured him. "Everything is going to be okay. Lay your head down, don't you worry now."

In his hospital room, doctors ran in and out while prepping James for surgery. The movements became a blur, and James started to drift off. "Was this the end?" he wondered as his heavy lids finally shut. . . Seconds turned into minutes, and minutes turned into hours, as doctors operated to save his life.

"James, James! Can you hear me? Can you hear me, my dear?" His mother's stern tone came through the fog.

Was that his finger that moved? It was! James was alive!

"Praise the Lord!" his mother bellowed from the top of her lungs, dancing as if everything was suddenly right in the world.

The corner of James's mouth curled up. The lead doctor came into the room to inform him he had to remove one of his lungs and how lucky he was to be alive. "Mate, if it weren't for the 13 blood transfusions of a handful of generous people, you wouldn't be alive right now." (That is the equivalent to nearly three and a half *gallons* of blood!)

Over the next three and a half months, while recovering in his hospital bed, James vowed that when he was old enough, he would donate his blood to thank the random strangers who saved his life that day. He knew he was alive for a reason and a purpose.

Fast-forward four years to 1955 as James celebrated his birthday with family and close friends. "I'm going to go give blood tomorrow. I'm a man now, I'm 18. I promised I would. And I can't break my promise. Mum, can you take me to the hospital tomorrow?"

"Sure thing, dear, I would be honored to," his mother chimed in peacefully, just happy James was celebrating his 18th birthday alive.

However, James was harboring a secret. As much as he wanted to give blood and keep his word, he had a strong aversion to needles. He was deathly afraid of them, even to the point of passing out. Deep down, he didn't want to give blood. He didn't want anything to do with it. But he knew he needed to keep his word.

The next morning, the hospital doors opened with a swoosh and James felt his heart drum a little faster. He wondered if he'd actually be able to go through with the promise he made. It's one thing to *say* he'd donate blood in the moments immediately following a life-saving surgery, but to actually *do* it, to take a needle to the vein, that was the part that made him sweat.

What if he ran out now? No one would blame him, right? What're a few pints of blood anyways? It's not like his blood was going to save a specific person's life, the hospital already had plenty of blood stored up from others.

James could practically feel the color drain from his face as the nurse wrapped his upper arm with banded pressure. He scanned the room, measuring the distance from his cold chair to the open door that signaled freedom. He could rip off his bandage and make a dash for the exit in two seconds flat; this was his chance. It was now or never. Now. Or never.

"James, are you okay?" His mother asked. He didn't say a word. He couldn't. He was too focused on not passing out. His face pinched tight, eyes squeezed shut, and right on cue, the tip of the needle broke skin. Tried as he might, his gaze couldn't help but drift to the tubes. He watched as his blood filled each vial to the brim, one after another. Could he spare this much blood? Was he giving too much? Every muscle in his body tensed. He was ready to run. Then, suddenly . . . it was over.

"See, that wasn't so bad now, was it?" the nurse asked as she pulled the needle from his arm. All James could manage was a nod. He'd survived, and that's what mattered.

James continued to give blood for the next 10 years, a couple of times every month. He made good on his word, and then some. Eventually, he didn't mind taking the needle in his arm. He had found his purpose. His life had been spared, and he was going to do the same for others. All was copasetic.

Then one day when James was 28 years old, he strolled into the hospital to give a routine blood donation. Instead of being met by the usual friendly nurse, James was greeted by a doctor, ushered into a hospital room, and asked to wait there.

"Doctor, come in here! Now! Hurry!" the doctor barked at the hospital's lead doctor.

What was it? What about James's scheduled blood draw could be so crucial it required such attention? He was curious, but worried.

"James, sit down, please; we have something important to discuss," the lead doctor said in a soft, mellow tone as he crossed the room.

"James, we have good news and bad news. It's something we discovered from the blood you donated two weeks ago. Let me start you off with the good news first. When a woman is pregnant, the baby's blood can enter the mother's bloodstream. And this is okay if they both have Rh-positive blood.

But if they don't, it can be deadly to the babies. Rhesus disease (Rh disease) is a condition caused by an incompatibility between the blood of a mother and that of her fetus. Eighty-five percent of mothers are Rh-positive, which means the baby will likely have a normal birth. However, the 15% of mothers who are Rh-negative, that's a different story. If the mother is Rh-negative and her fetus is Rh-positive, the mother's body will produce antibodies to fight off the baby's Rh-positive blood. It recognizes the foreign blood cells as something to be destroyed. If the baby makes it to full term, he or she will be born extremely ill and likely have major complications their entire life."

The doctor paused. "Okay," James said, still without any idea where the doctor was going with this.

"James, you have the only blood the world has ever seen that is capable of preventing this disease. We can't explain exactly how this happened but in the blood transfusions that saved your life, your plasma must have developed unusually strong and persistent antibodies against the D Rh group antigen. It's a wonder you are still alive and healthy. We've never seen anything like it before; you have a gift that could save millions of babies' lives."

"Millions of lives?" James thought. His blood could help save *millions* of lives? No way could this be true.

"James," the doctor said, snapping him back to reality.

"I wish I could stop there at the good news. The bad news is, this isn't going to be easy; your life will be at risk. We would need you to switch over to making blood plasma donations. And lots of them. There is a possibility that when we do this, you won't be the same. You could live your life with extremely low energy, constantly feeling drained and sick, and possibly even live a life cut short of many years. I know this is a lot to take in. But, remember, you could save the lives of millions of unborn babies. We will give you some time to think it over."

James sat alone in the hospital room as if in a trance. What just happened? How could this be true? Was he chosen to save millions?

And what if they were wrong? What if taking his blood plasma wouldn't save lives but would only lead to his death? Could he really go through with this and risk living a scarcer or shortened life?

THE CRUX

Does James accept what the doctor told him and give his precious blood for the opportunity to save millions of strangers' lives? Or does he hold on to his blood, keeping it for himself because he fears scarcity?

***

Have you ever heard the tiny voice in the back of your head taunting you, "You'll never get what you want!" The audible pounding from eardrum to eardrum continues to get louder to the point it becomes deafening, yet you can't stop the vibration. The voice isn't a scream, but instead, it is a snake in the garden—conniving and manipulating. The snake whispers "If you try, you will fail; 99% of people do. And even if you happen to succeed in the moment, you will eventually lose it all and regret ever trying."

Before you know it, you are knee-deep in the quicksand of self-doubt.

"What if I invest and I lose it all?"

Better not take the chance.

"What if I go all in on my dreams and fall flat on my face?"

Why even try?

"It's never going to work, I'm never going to make it, there's not enough to go around," the lies continue.

Hold on to what you have.

You've heard horror stories of those who made money and then lost it all. What were they thinking? Why didn't they just quit while they were ahead?

You're not crazy for thinking this way. It's how we've been conditioned to think—by the media, by society. You could turn on the news at any given moment and the headlines would read something to the effect of "Food shortage supply inevitable in the near future." "US utility operator warns of the day when we won't have any water left to drink." "Stock your homes with toilet paper before stores run out."

The world doesn't want you to know the truth. If you knew these horrific "possibilities" weren't actually going to happen, how could they keep you under their control? They couldn't!

But even just having the thought of losing it all makes you sick to your stomach. So you hold everything close. Very close. But instead of this making you feel safe like you were striving so hard to do, you feel consumed. Consumed with fear.

Taking action, that's a risk. And to you, risks may lead to being broke and living on the street. You make fun of the TV shows about hoarding, the people who have boxes on boxes of stuff scattered throughout their house. But without even knowing it, you have become one of them, stockpiling away possibilities and opportunities.

A *scarcity mindset* is an obsession with a lack of something—usually time, money, or opportunities. You can't seem to focus on anything else, no matter how hard you try.

Imagine a freshly baked pumpkin pie sitting on the table in front of you; it has been cut into many slices. These hypothetical slices represent the number of opportunities available to anyone who is in your field of work. You *have* to hold on tightly to the slice served to you, right?

Wrong.

Arguably the greatest action taker to ever walk the planet, Jesus, said it best in the parable of the talents.

Matthew 25: 15–26

15 To one he gave five talents, to another two, to another one, to each according to his ability. Then he went away. **16** He who had received the five talents went at once and traded with them, and he made five talents more. **17** So also he who had the two talents made two talents more. **18** But he who had received the one talent went and dug in the ground and hid his master's money.

20 And he who had received the five talents came forward, bringing five talents more, saying, "Master, you delivered to me five talents; here, I have made five talents more." **21** His master said to him, "Well done, good and faithful servant. You have been faithful over a little; I will set you over much. Enter into the joy of your master."

24 He also who had received the one talent came forward, saying, "Master, I knew you to be a hard man, reaping where you did not sow, and gathering where you scattered no seed, **25** so I was afraid, and I went and hid your talent in the ground. Here, you have what is yours." **26** But his master answered him, "You wicked and slothful servant! You knew that I reap where I have not sown and gather where I scattered no seed? **27** Then you ought to have invested my money with the bankers, and at my coming I should have received what was my own with interest." **28** So take the talent from him and give it to him who has the ten talents. **29** For to everyone who has will more be given, and he will have an abundance. But from the one who has not, even what he has will be taken away. **30** And cast the worthless servant into the outer darkness. In that place there will be weeping and gnashing of teeth.

Why do I put the parable of the talents in this book? It's simply to show you how costly it is to *not* curate your God-given ability, aka talents.

Now I'm not saying go out and invest your time and money recklessly. What I am saying is that you have a gift to use, not bury. You have a gift to have an impact on the lives of others. But if you hold that gift tightly to your chest, afraid to lose it, you are actually being selfish—extremely selfish. It's like owning a pair of the most beautiful shoes but keeping them buried in a box deep in the closet out of fear they might get dirty. By doing this, they are never used for their intended purpose.

The Brain

Now let's see what the brain has to say about the scarcity *mindset*. Studies have shown that just by the brain operating in the scarcity mindset, your IQ can lower by 14 points. Now that might not sound like a lot, but 14 IQ points can take you from the efficiency level to the deficiency level. It's a dramatic drop in IQ.

Scarcity mindset is *risk aversion*. Knowing the journey might be difficult. You would much rather play it safe to avoid any pain or loss than bet on yourself, even if the potential gain could be life changing. In other words, the thought of losing what you have outweighs the thought of any gain.

Imagine you have the opportunity to invest a couple thousand dollars.

A. You could instead invest that money in the stock market, but the prognosticators are saying it could crash at any minute.

B. You could invest that money into a real estate property knowing the physical asset will provide long-term ROI. However, there is a rumbling of a housing market crash in the near future.

C. You could invest it in yourself to learn the tools that could multiply your business by ten times. But that feels even riskier, and there's no promised guarantee you will see the direct ROI, so you pass.

D. None of the above

The fear of volatility wins out. You choose D.

"I can't invest it in myself, I can't invest it in the markets, so I might as well just put it into a savings account. I can't lose it there, right?" That's what we are taught to think until you realize inflation over time causes you to actually *lose* money in a savings account. So much for playing it safe, huh?

In an interesting study done by LaFreniere and Newman, 29 undergraduate students were analyzed to determine just how many of their worries really came true over the course of three weeks. On average, 91.39% of participants' worries did NOT come true (i.e., only 8.61% of their worries DID come true).

So wait, more than nine out of ten of your worries *won't* come true? But yet, you continue to think the exact opposite. Let it go already, the scarcity mindset will only guarantee you live a scarcity life. That's the truth. If you are one of the one-tenth in which the worst case does occur, consider yourself lucky. Lucky because you will make it through, and I know you will learn and grow from it in the process.

"A smooth sea never made a skilled sailor."
—Franklin D. Roosevelt

It's freeing to know it is factually proven that our worst-case scenarios more than likely won't come true. And if that's not convincing enough, it gets even better. We can all agree we would never say no to more time and more money, correct? According to the same study, on average, participants found that worrying took up 25.88% of their thinking time each day. So not only are these worst-case scenarios not happening, they are also taking up *a quarter* of our waking hours worrying about the what-ifs.

Think about how much more you could get done by adding that time back into your day. And all it takes is letting go of the scarcity mindset. Oh, but wait, we're not done yet.

If less worry and more time weren't convincing enough evidence for you, let's take a look at personal stress levels. According to the same study, worst-case scenario thinking has a significant emotional cost as well. During the early part of the study, participants reported an average distress rating of 4.51 out of 7 (i.e., a moderate to high level of distress).

So let me break this down for you as plain and simple as possible: nine out of ten of your worst-case scenario thoughts will not come true. If instead of investing in yourself, you hold on to your money and put it all in savings, your money will devalue. If you worry about the worst-case scenario playing out, you will have 25% less time in your day. Oh, *and* your stress levels will be significantly higher.

Scarcity mindset seems like quite the utopia, huh?

The Heart

You hold on to what you have because you are afraid of losing it (in other words: you fear failure).

> What if you go broke?
>
> What if you can't pay rent?
>
> What if you end up living on the street?

It's hard to take action. It can seem daunting. I get it. We don't know if the risk (action) we take will lead to the reward. That's common human nature.

So why not stay just in your comfort zone? Because the *comfort zone* is a lie. The American Dream is a lie. You work 9–5, put in your time, buy a house, have 2½ kids, work until you can retire—that's just being another robot in the system. And one thing I know to be true: God did *not* create you to "go through the motions."

> Thinking about starting a business or pursuing your dream? Don't do it. You'll lose a lot of money and maybe even go into debt.
>
> Thinking about hiring a personal coach to help you sharpen your skills and your mission? Naw, probably shouldn't. What if you don't make the money back you invested? Not worth the risk.
>
> Throw that way of thinking out the window now! The heart can't take the stress that your constant worry and scarcity mentality is putting it through!

According to a 2018 report from the *Global Entrepreneurship Monitor*, roughly one-third of entrepreneurs didn't start a business because of fear of failure. At least they won't have to taste failure. But, they'll also never taste success. Your heart grows through failure. The heart muscle strengthens when you fail.

A study conducted by Northwestern University's Kellogg School of Management analyzed data from scientists who applied for grants early in their careers. They categorized them based on those who received funding for research (the "success group") and those who didn't (the "failure group"). Then, they tracked how many papers those scientists published over the next decade and how many times their studies were cited in other articles to gauge their success. Those in the failure group were *6.1% more likely* to publish a high-impact paper than those in the success group.

The ones who failed became more likely to succeed. Doesn't that seem contradictory? No. Because failure grows the heart stronger. An un-failed heart is a delicate heart.

Your heart is also inherently selfish. *Schadenfreude* is when someone derives pleasure from witnessing (or learning about) another person's misfortune. Your heart views *others' success* as a precursor to *fewer* opportunities for you. You automatically think, "Well, if *they* achieved the sale or [fill in the blank with the success metric in your field of work], then there will be less for me." And even if on the surface you cheer on others' success; in reality, the burning sensation in your heart screams out "If they succeed, then there isn't enough room for me!"

Caught yourself thinking that before?

Yeah, I thought so. So why is it that hamburger restaurants like McDonalds, Burger King, and Wendy's, on average, do better overall when they are in close proximity to one another than they do if they are the only option in the vicinity?

Demand. They are all able to thrive because there is a known demand for a burger in that area. Think about it, if someone in your field of work is "killing it," don't you think that might just mean there is a demand for your line of work? Of course, it does!

Stop living out *schadenfreude* and start being *magnanimous*.

What if you decide from this day forward to genuinely cheer on others' successes? What if you look at the success of others as a success for you? What if you stop protecting your heart as if it's The Hope Diamond and begin refuting all the lies a scarcity mindset has misled you with over the years?

I just had a slice of pumpkin pie, apple pie, and even a piece of cheesecake with ice cream on top. Will you?

What Actually Happened to James Harrison?

James Harrison sat perched on the edge of the lab room chair. Part of him wanted to run, the weight of the decision seemed too heavy. His life, or the lives of potentially millions? And he had the power to choose.

"Why did you ever vow to give blood in the first place?" he muttered to himself under his breath. He knew the answer. To save lives, just like his had been saved. Even if his life was on the line, yet again, he couldn't turn back now.

So, James put aside his fear of scarcity, took action, and the results were staggering. James Harrison's blood was unique so it was used to develop the first known injection of Anti-D immunoglobulin, which fights against and significantly reduces the chances of a baby contracting Rhesus (Rh) disease. Mothers are now able to go into pregnancy confident that even if their babies contract Rhesus, they will survive. So not only has James saved babies' lives but also spared millions of mothers from the depression that losing their child in the womb would cause. Mothers can now go into pregnancy with peace of mind.

Before James, there was no cure. James had a very clear choice. Nobody forced him to do anything. It would have been understandable even for him to want to save every bit of his blood to ensure he lived a healthy, long life. But James chose to see the survival and success of another human life as a success for himself. He allowed doctors to draw out rich plasma and did so every single week, giving as much blood as the doctors needed. Think about that, even when James might have felt inclined to not give blood (as every draw potentially put his own life at risk), he still insisted on doing so. Every single batch of Anti-D originates from James Harrison.

That is 1,173 blood donations given by James Harrison over 60 years saving 2.4 million babies.

In 1999, James Harrison was awarded "Man of the Year" title in Australia and is forever known as "The Man with the Golden Arm." Despite the risk that donating his precious blood could backfire and lead to an early death, James took action and gave blood. And he did so every single week until he "retired" at 81, the age at which donations are no longer medically allowed.

FLIP THE SCRIPT

You wake up on a Thursday morning on vacation in Hawaii. Ah, the peace of the morning breeze off the ocean lowers your blood pressure on impact. You check your phone out of habit.

Twenty missed calls. "Twenty?!" you think as your heart begins to race. Half of those calls are from your parents, the other half are from your older brother.

"What on earth could be going on?" Your mind jumps to every possible worst-case scenario. You call your mother back immediately.

"What is going on?!" you ask without giving her a chance to even say hello.

"It's your sister. She gave birth early," she responds in a melancholic tone. "The baby boy's not doing well."

"Well, what's the issue? Talk to me, what's wrong with him?" you ask, now becoming increasingly nervous to hear your mother's answer.

"The doctors don't think he's going to make it. He has Rhesus disease and is losing blood rapidly. He is already showing signs of possible brain damage. He needs a blood transfusion but they can't find anyone with a match to donate."

"What are we going to do?" you ask in a panic.

"There is nothing we can do," your mother responds miserably.

"I'll give my blood," you pronounce as if you have found the missing piece of a 1,000-piece puzzle. But your efforts are futile. The transfusion is needed immediately and besides that, your blood isn't a match for the baby's. His life now depends on the donations of strangers.

Time is not on his side, or yours. You quickly flip open your laptop to learn everything you can about what Rhesus disease is and why there isn't something to treat it. You could have sworn that in college you learned about a man who donated his blood and it prevented this from happening. But as you search Google, all that comes up are one tragic story after another of mothers and their sick babies.

This is because James Harrison never took action. He decided not to donate his blood plasma. He just couldn't move past his fear and scarcity mindset. Because of this, it was impossible for anyone to ever create an Anti-D injection. Now, 2.4 million humans don't exist because they either died in the womb or shortly after birth.

With a scarcity mindset, you will never find fulfillment. There will always be *something* you are trying to protect from losing. But abundance never comes through holding on; it only arrives when you *let go*. The cause of poverty is not scarcity; the cause of poverty is fear. That which is empty, can receive. I'm sure you have heard "pour, pour, and pour into others and it will all come back to you in return." It will. Trust me, it will. Plant the seeds of abundance and the tree of life will grow.

Matthew 16:26
  For what is a man profited, if he shall gain the whole world, and lose his own soul?

What you hold on to will be lost.

But what you give, that will be forever gained.

TOOLS TO OVERCOME THE SCARCITY MINDSET

There is more than enough to go around for everyone. Repeat that sentence out loud.

The economy will crash; you will go broke and lose it forever if you don't hold onto your money. You won't. Do a quick Google search on companies started during recessions or depressions and you will see what I mean.

Here is a brief list: Disney, Hyatt, Microsoft, HP, Airbnb, Uber, Electronic Arts, to name a few.

There is always enough, and there will always *be* enough. I know that's not natural nor is it a popular thought to believe. You now know the tricks your brain will play on you: "The worst-case scenario will happen this time, it's safer to be risk averse." And you know the reasons your heart wants to protect you: "Failure can't hurt you if you don't even start."

You know *why* you have the scarcity mindset; now it's time for me to show you how to conquer this archetype.

The 1% Abundance

According to a 2021 CNBC Study, 73% of Americans rank *finances* as their number-one stressor.

Now, the premise of this book isn't to tell you *how* to manage your money. But, the following tool could absolutely make all the difference in freeing your mind from the stronghold that financial strain may have on you, and ultimately show you how to release the scarcity mindset from all other areas of your life.

I can honestly say this tool has been one of the most impactful, positive habits I've made toward living a life of abundance and my overall peace of mind. It is that important.

I used to think, "Well, if I work hard for the money I earn, then the money is mine and I'm going to hold on tight to it. God forbid I give any of it away."

That was my way of thinking for 28 years.

And then I discovered give and you will get more in return— a concept that was an exact contradiction to what I had always thought to be true.

I began to *tithe*. And I know this word can rub people the wrong way; I felt that way at one point, too. The word in general just seems to make most people uncomfortable.

But I tried it. I started small, very small. Just 1% per month of my total income. And then 2%, then 3%. I'll be the first to tell you, it wasn't easy. I would see the money I worked so hard for go away with a click of an online donation button.

But after a while, something wild happened. Out of nowhere I started receiving more offers to run basketball camps, more NBA players asking to be trained, and more team consulting deals, and these offers were substantially more than I had been making prior to my tithing.

I couldn't believe it. So, I began to give more: 4%, 5%, all the way up to the 14% I give today.

Now, I'm not saying you need to give 14%, but I do challenge you to start out small and work your way up to at least 10%. Of all the "successful wealthy people" I know, they *all* tithe. Every single one of them. Must be something to this *letting go* that equals abundance.

In a CDC Capital study in 2013, people who reported tithing 10% or more were half as likely to have overdue credit card statements than those who didn't tithe. The study also found only 28% of tithers were in some type of financial debt. Now this might sound like a high number to you, until you compare it to the percentage of all Americans who are in financial debt: 77%. So approximately 190 million Americans are in debt, only approximately 1.5 million Americans tithe, so that means only .0022% of the American population are tithers who are in debt.

Speaking from personal experience, I no longer have a strained relationship with money. I think it's important to point out that when I first started my business, I had nothing in my bank account. For years I slept either in Walmart parking lots or on friends' couches as I lived paycheck to paycheck and out of my car as I drove across the country to work small-town basketball camps. So, there was definitely a time when counting every single penny was normal for me. And it's also important to share that I began tithing *before* I was making any substantial profits at my job. Doing this was really, *really* uncomfortable for me. But as I stuck with it, it freed my mind up in other areas of my life apart from just finances: I now refer sponsorship offers to friends instead of hoarding them for myself. I offer speaking engagement opportunities to friends instead of thinking they are all only for me.

I don't say this to toot my own horn; I say this because it's the honest truth and I want the lessons I've already learned to help save you anymore time wasted in a scarcity mindset.

Action step for the day: Start small with 1%. Give 1% of your monthly income this month to your church, or favorite charity or nonprofit. Then try 2% the following month. And if you need to stay there for a while, that's okay! But make it a goal to work your way up to 10% eventually within the upcoming year. And if you *don't* see abundance pour into your life, please message me and tell me I'm full of sh**.

I strongly believe that implementing this tool into your life will dramatically help you live a more abundant and fulfilled life.

Double Decker á la Mode

Imagine you have a freshly baked pumpkin pie sitting on the table in front of you.

Now imagine that pie represents the field of work you are in.

For me, the pie itself represents the speaking industry. Let's say the pie can be sliced into 30 slices. These slices represent the number of keynote events throughout the year. This means there are only 30 slices in total and every other motivational speaker is vying for a piece. Competition is fierce to say the least.

Now, if I view the speaking pie with an everyone-for-themselves mindset and try to gobble up as many slices as quickly as possible, I would pass out in a food coma. I might have held onto the pieces I wanted, but in the process, I exhausted myself. I temporarily felt like I gained, but in reality, I missed out because I was asleep. The point here is, I got *my* slices, didn't allow anyone else to touch them, and in the end, I had nothing more to show for it.

But now let's say I come up with an idea for the pumpkin pie that allows me and my fellow speakers to have even more pie than what we originally thought was the maximum number of slices. We wouldn't have to fight over the slices. In fact, we could each have just the perfect amount and take home as many leftovers as possible to last us for much longer than a temporary moment. Nor would I feel the urgency to eat myself into a coma.

My idea: create a two-layer pie. What's better than one layer? Two layers.

So the pie (speaking industry) can actually have more than the 30 slices? Absolutely. What I thought was the *limit* originally was actually just me living in a scarcity mindset.

Rather than only relying on my agent to get me gigs, I invited a few of my speaking *competitors* to collaborate with me to put on smaller in-person events that provided us all with additional opportunities and income. And on top of that, I went *á la mode* style by reaching out to companies and negotiating Zoom talks. My agent didn't hand these opportunities to me. I went out and created them myself and with the help of the people I typically would have considered to be the people I wanted to take pieces from. *Á la* mode gives you the freedom to think outside the box (the pie) of your given industry and create new ventures. These events generated *new* revenue (more slices of the pie), and set the groundwork for relationships that would provide reoccurring opportunities instead of just one-and-done deals. My agent is amazing and gets me wonderful gigs, but if you rely solely on being handed slices, your mind will automatically live in a scarcity mode.

This can *only* be done if you live with an abundance mindset.

The point of this tool is to realize that life and opportunities do not have to be limited.

Rather, they are limitless. You have the ability to collaborate and create new opportunities. You can even recommend others for opportunities and maybe they will do the same in return for me sometime. However, even if they don't, you can feel confident knowing you provided value to someone else, and the return will ultimately come back to you in a bigger way than you can imagine.

Action for the day: This one could get messy, and tasty. Very tasty.

I want you to plan an evening this week with your family to buy or make a pie. It can be any type of pie, but make sure you start off with only the base (pumpkin, apple, cherry, etc.). Then go crazy and get creative. You can add a layer of cake to the pie, ice cream, toppings, whatever you want until your heart is content. The challenge is to see how high you can build the pie. And while you do this, talk with your spouse and/or kids about how they can proactively serve others in their same *competitive* field (classmates, sports teammates vying for playing time). Show them there is always enough if they give, and when they do it will all come back to them and then some (and be prepared for a potential food coma afterwards!).

YOUR ACTION ANIMAL: THE MEERKAT

You will never see a lone meerkat in the wild. Why? Because it cannot survive on its own.

Meerkats might appear small and always in survival mode (made famous by Timon in the *Lion King*). But don't be fooled: meerkats working together are some of the most productive species ruling the desert lands.

Source: stanciuc/Adobe Stock

It's no wonder a group of meerkats is referred to as a *gang*. Each member of the gang has a role, and all roles are of equal importance. Whether the role is to be the babysitter of the young, the sentry soldier watching for potential danger, or the lead gatherer sent out to collect food for the day, the meerkats' collaboration ensures the group not only survives but thrives.

The meerkat gang is transient by nature because they can't store food for more than a day at a time. Their lean bodies don't allow them the luxury of stored fat. (You probably wish you were a meerkat in that manner, huh?)

Meerkats have unconditional *trust* in their gang. There is no disdain toward another's role, there is no jealousy that one meerkat's position of rank might be "more important" than the others, and there is no ability to retain what they have, afraid they will lose it all.

Adopt the mantra of the meerkat. As Timon, famously told Simba in the *Lion King*: "Hakuna Matata—it means no worries for the rest of your days."

"This is one title I don't want to hold onto. It's the only record I hope is broken. Because if they do, that means someone gave even more."
                    —James Harrison, after making the *Guinness Book of World Records* for his donations

---

CHAPTER 8

The Distracted

Meet Isaac Newton

"You're late again," Isaac's professor sighed.

"I'm sorry, Mrs. Brown. It won't happen again," Isaac promised, fumbling through his knapsack for his book.

"Take a seat," she instructed, pointing to the back of the room.

Punctuality and Isaac rarely go hand in hand. Scattered, distracted, and preoccupied would be a far better description for the bright senior at Cambridge University with a mind fond of wandering.

There was no denying Isaac was smart but his head was always in the clouds—present physically (when he was on time) but never mentally. His brain had no brake. His mind often ran on overdrive, stuck on a never-ending carnival ride of thoughts and distractions, thoughts and distractions. When he wasn't working his brain into the ground, he was saying yes to every opportunity and endeavor that came his way, filling his plate with a hodgepodge of attention thieves. His grades plummeted. Only a few classes shy of graduating, if Isaac didn't turn things around stat, graduation wouldn't be an option.

On a crisp fall morning in 1665, Isaac was summoned to the chancellor's office to discuss his progress. "You can come in now," the chancellor motioned to Isaac, who stood staring aimlessly off into space as he waited outside the office, no doubt lost in another daydream about his latest project. Daydreaming and Isaac, now *that* went hand in hand.

"Isaac!" the chancellor raised his voice.

"Yes sir, yes sir, I'm coming," Isaac stuttered, snapping out of his trance.

The potential the chancellor once saw in Isaac during his admissions interview had all but vanished. And Isaac's follow-through was a must. After all, not just anyone is accepted into Cambridge: only the most promising young minds throughout all of England were given the prestigious opportunity.

"What's going on, son? I know you are a smart kid, but you're failing two of your classes, and if you don't pass them both, I won't be able to allow you to graduate."

Isaac quickly nodded, promising compliance. He reached for his bag eager to get out of there.

"Hold on, not so fast. Sit for a second more. I need to tell you something important." Isaac's heart jumped straight to his throat. He braced for bad news. "Isaac, you need to learn how to focus. What good does it do to be as smart as you are if you aren't able to apply your abilities?"

The chancellor let the question hang there as Isaac chewed on the words.

"Is he right?" Isaac thought. "Will I never amount to anything because I have too much on my plate?" Isaac's shoulders drooped. He simply nodded and the chancellor motioned toward the door, letting him know he was excused. Deflated, Isaac made his way back to his room, slugging through campus as he pondered his life. "Am I trying to do too much?" He wondered as he kicked the ground, sending a flutter of scarlet and gold leaves into the air. Failing, yes. Distracted, definitely. Stressed, very.

Even from a young age, Isaac struggled to buckle down and focus on a single task for any extended period. His frustrations over this eventually surfaced by way of a temper. His lack of concentration led to stress and stress led to anger and anger to rage. All because his distracted mind could never find the off switch.

Days later, with finals just around the corner, word spread through Cambridge that students were falling ill. A new disease, unknown to anyone before, was sweeping the student body.

"What is it?" Isaac asked his roommate, who looked as if he'd just seen a ghost.

"Cambridge is shutting down!" He yelled, gasping for breath.

"What? Shutting down?" Isaac questioned.

"It's called the Black Plague and it's spreading like wildfire. Supposed to be deadly, too. The chancellor is sending everyone home until it clears," his roommate revealed.

Was this a blessing in disguise? Had Isaac's ticket to freedom from failing out of Cambridge just been handed to him? Isaac felt elated, swept away by a wave of pure joy. But it wasn't long until a cloud of doubt and uncertainty soon followed.

"Well, what am I going to do? Go home? I won't have the means there to do everything I need to do. I'm going to be so bored," he thought, an internal battle brewing. He had no choice; everyone had to retreat to their homes for fear the Black Plague would spread.

As Isaac traveled home to Woolsthorpe Manor, he was torn. Yes, he was thankful he didn't have to face the ramifications of flunking out, but he was worried about how he'd spend his time at home. He had been raised by his grandparents, who lived on a farm in the middle of nowhere. There would be nothing to do, and stillness scared Isaac almost more than the widening pandemic.

"Welcome home, dear," Isaac's grandmother greeted him at the doorstep with a warm embrace. "I'm just so happy you're safe and healthy. Your grandfather and I were so worried about you, you know that? And you're almost graduated, I know you will when school opens back up again. This will be a good time to unwind. Right, Isaac?" His grandmother questioned. Unwind? Isaac loathed the thought.

"Right, sure, grandma," he said with a forced smile, placating her. Inside, Isaac's stomach was a tangle of knots. What would he do with his time? He wanted to pursue alchemy, he wanted to work on his seven different projects, he wanted to study Greek philosophy, he wanted to keep up with the news he was used to in the city, and he wanted to do it all. But, he was stuck on a farm in complete obscurity, separated from everything that made him tick.

"Grandpa, can I speak with you?" Isaac asked peering around the corner into his office. Isaac's grandfather was a stern man of few words. But Isaac respected him and looked to him for wisdom. "What should I do?" Isaac asked timidly. "I want to do so many different things, but I just can't here. It's driving me nuts, Pa," Isaac said with strain in his voice.

His grandfather measured his response. "Isaac, sometimes when you want to get somewhere quickly, you must first go slow. The trees in the field grow tall and wide, but do you ever see them sprouting in such a hurry? Let your roots grow, son, let your roots grow."

Isaac digested his grandfather's words. Half inspired, half confused. As profound as that statement sounded, Isaac didn't quite understand what his grandfather was trying to tell him.

Later that night, while on the hunt for a distraction, Isaac paused and heard his grandfather's words echo in his head: "To get somewhere quickly, you must first go slow." Slow. Was that it? Did Isaac need to slow down and pause? Had his life become so hectic, so full of distractions, that he couldn't see the light through the constant cloud of stimulation? "But how could that be?" Isaac thought. "Won't slowing down waste time?"

He could admit that perhaps he needed to tweak his time management and dedicate more to the classes he was failing, but other than that, he was accomplishing much more than any other student he knew. They were all only growing in one or two areas. But Isaac was extremely well-rounded and had his foot in every project, subject, and activity imaginable. Wasn't that the way to get ahead in the long run? Surely, he could just continue doing what he was doing, and eventually, he would be caught up and then get ahead in every single pursuit.

But his grandfather's words, "The trees in the field grow tall and wide," continued to play in his head on repeat as he lay in bed staring at the ceiling.

Was his grandfather right? Did he, Isaac Newton, need to slow down and give his racing mind a breather to actually discover what he was meant to do?

THE CRUX

Does Isaac Newton follow the suggestion to slow down and take a break from the mental racing and constant distraction that emotionally was driving him nuts? Or did he stay on his "mission to do everything" mentality that was causing him stress?

***

Your alarm goes off on your phone at 6:14 am. You roll over in bed, still half asleep, and swat at the nightstand until your hand hits your screen. Blinking groggily, you look at your phone to turn it off and you see the different notification banners. Thirty-four unread messages, six new WhatsApp notifications, 26 new emails, seven Instagram DMs, three missed calls, a notification of a past-due credit card statement, and calendar reminders for the six meetings you have today.

Your heart beats faster. And faster. And faster. Growing tenfold, to the point that all you want to do is crawl back under the covers and hide from the world! Overwhelm grips its claws, as you maneuver your way out of bed thinking about your overdue credit card bill and the email your boss sent about the sales report that was supposed to be in his inbox yesterday.

This is never the life you wanted. You didn't want to be the person who got on the hamster wheel and could never get off. Not you. But that is now your reality.

As you grab breakfast with one hand and scramble to type out emails on your phone with the other, the thought pops into your head, "Does life really have to be like this? Do I actually have to let these notifications rule my life?

"Could there be a life where I have time for my kids, where I have time to work on passion projects that truly excite me, *and* where I have time to just sit on my porch and be present with the birds chirping in nature? Is that utopia just a Mother Goose fairytale?"

How many times has this scenario, or something very similar, played out in your own life? We are living in the most *distracted* era in human history. There is never enough time; we are always too busy. There are way too many options to choose from and our minds are constantly running on hyperdrive, overloaded by distractions.

Ask yourself this question: When was the last time you opened Netflix and realized 45 minutes later you were still searching for a show to watch? Never before have on our minds been kamikaze bombed with so many things battling for our attention. We all need a personal assistant just to handle our distractions!

But why are we so distracted?

The Brain

Psychologists Matthew Killingsworth and Daniel Gilbert found that the human mind is wired for a state of continuous distraction. Because our brains are hardwired with survival instincts, they are accustomed to interference. Years ago, when our ancestors sensed trouble, their brains kicked into a distracted fight-or-flight mode. Today, our 86 billion neurons have acclimated to processing information every second as we numbly scroll through social media.

In Killingsworth and Gilbert's study conducted with 2,250 adults, they concluded that we spend around 47% of every waking hour "mind wandering" aka *distracted*. Mind wandering, also referred to as *stimulus-independent thought*, has become an experience so natural we don't even notice it.

You're sitting at the office daydreaming about the cruise you wish you were on. You're in a dinner conversation with a client, but all you can think about are the emails you forgot to send earlier. The human mind is wired to *drift*.

You are waging a war in your mind not on the battlefield of *time management*, but instead on *attention management*. We all have the same amount of time in a day, the difference is in how it is filtered and focused. Think about it this way: every piece of information that goes into your brain is automatically run through a filtration process.

This filtration flows directly into your decision-making process. If your filtration process is constantly clogged up with distractions, then the information processing stops there. This pattern makes distracted living your default mode. Fewer chances to make decisions on incoming information means fewer chances to take action.

Let's get really brainy here and see exactly how the *distraction* process works. The process originates in the prefrontal cortex, which is connected to a region in the brain known as the striatum—an area that suppresses visual input. The striatum then sends input to a region called the globus pallidus, which is part of the basal ganglia. The basal ganglia then suppresses activation in the part of the thalamus that processes visual information.

Confused? Don't worry, I'll show you why this all matters.

In the early 1900s, Prussian scientists discovered the brain has rhythms and that the rhythms alter between two different brain states: one that is associated with focus and one that is associated with distractibility.

The groundbreaking findings showed convincing evidence that brain rhythms can be linked very closely to our behavioral outcomes.

So why is this so important? Our brain goes through rapid responses subconsciously at such a fast rate. However, this is the same decision-making process that is responsible for our survival.

A car speeding directly toward you, a child in a stroller rolling into a busy intersection—our rapid responses are what keep us alive! They are our greatest survival mechanism.

But if your brain's rhythms are clogged with distraction, as the brain regions experience reduced visual input, the synapses in your brain will no longer fire at the same speed they need to be functioning at to keep us out of harm's way.

Society, through distraction, is slowly devolving in the opposite direction of "survival of the fittest."

But is the real culprit of your overly distracted life actually external? Sure, you can blame the 3.04 million apps on your phone, the 667,865 restaurants in your area, the 532 channels you are able to watch, not to mention the 64 different streaming services.

But is the real reason you are distracted something you can blame on the outside world? A closer look at the heart will tell.

The Heart

The real culprit isn't external irritations, but rather an internal urge to be distracted. Wait, what? Why would we *want* to be distracted?

Imagine this scenario: you strip away all the distractions in your life, there are no more notifications, no more multitude of choices for every decision you need to make. What if all the external disturbances were suddenly gone? And what if who you found on the inside wasn't the person you wanted to see? What if the external distractions are, in fact, shields you hold up to dodge the reality of how you are choosing to live your life?

Nobody diagnosed this problem as brilliantly as Friedrich Nietzsche, the cantankerous nineteenth-century German philosopher who argued in *Unmodern Observations* that we seek out distractions to stay mentally busy, so we can avoid facing up to the big questions—like whether we're living genuinely meaningful lives.

Is that true in your life? Are you racing from one thing to the next in fear of having time to yourself to ponder? If you find one second of "free time," do you quickly pull out your phone to scroll through social media, check the news, or text a friend?

When was the last time you were out in nature alone with no phone, no cars, no civilization, and you were able to just take a deep breath and reflect on your life? At first, the stillness evokes a sense of relief, but then it's swiftly followed by the thoughts filling your mind of "What am I doing with my life? Am I wasting my life? Do I have a purpose?" It's a scary feeling and the easiest way to avoid having to face those questions is to indulge in the buffet of distractions.

Here are the two *Oxford Dictionary* definitions of the word *distraction*:

A thing that prevents someone from giving full attention to something else
   Extreme agitation of the mind or emotions

Does either of those apply to you? (If you didn't raise your hand; you are probably currently distracted!) I would answer yes and yes. And on a daily basis! We are living in a world that is more crammed with attention diversions than ever before. Ever. And it's not even close.

How did this happen? How did you wake up today unable to remember where the last ten years of your life went? Distractions. The evil game the world plays without you even knowing. And the reason you don't know is because you are too busy being distracted.

Let me hit you with some stats and let's see whether or not you agree this distraction thing is a real enemy to action. According to an *Inc. Magazine* study, 70% of workers who were surveyed admitted they feel distracted on the job. Yet 66% of those surveyed admitted they have never done anything to address it. Only 4% take action!!

According to a market study done by Winnick and Zolna, people on average touch their iPhones 2,617 times per day! (that's every 33 seconds over 24 hours). And according to Gloria Mark, who studies digital distraction at the University of California, Irvine, it takes on average 23 minutes and 15 seconds to return to your original task after the interruption occurs. You don't have to be a scholar to read between the lines and see distraction is destroying our society.

It's the epidemic no one wants to talk about—the *passenger on the ship of life* epidemic. Most human beings have given up on being the navigator for their ship of life, have unknowingly settled into the passenger seat, and have placed anything in their control on lifelong autopilot.

It's no wonder the obesity rate continues to rise year after year. No wonder the depression numbers are off the charts. No wonder 92% of people, the people we see every single day of our lives, never accomplish their dreams. We're too distracted to take action.

But it doesn't have to be like this. There's a better way, and I'm going to show you that way.

WHAT ACTUALLY HAPPENED TO ISAAC NEWTON?

Enlightenment came by way of a simple apple tree. Newton decided to embrace time in solitude. He went into nature, observed the animals and plants, pushed aside urges to fill his time with busy-work, and instead thought deeply about the things he had never had time for. Then one day, while sitting alone in the garden on his farm, Isaac saw an apple fall from a tree. Something so simple, yet something he had never had the time to take notice of before, provided him the inspiration that changed the entire course of his life.

The decision to be *still* led to the most productive and enlightening time of Newton's life, ultimately altering the trajectory of history as we know it.

With all the distractions of his previous lifestyle, Newton wouldn't have thought twice about the apple and instead would have eaten it as a snack.

Newton realized there was more to the falling fruit and began experimenting with gravity's pull, eventually shaping his most famous idea: the law of universal gravitation.

His first law of gravity stated that an object at rest stays at rest and an object in motion stays in motion with the same speed and in the same direction unless acted on by an unbalanced force. All thanks to making the time and space in solitude to allow an apple to fall on his head and think about why that occurred.

Isaac Newton revolutionized mathematics, geometry, and theories on gravity. He produced works of genius that changed the way the world operates. Like the invention of the reflecting telescope, which to this day gives everyday people the ability to see stars and planets in the night sky. Newton discovered what we know today as calculus. (If you had to take calculus in high school, you are probably not thanking Newton for that invention.) In his research book *Optiks*, he wrote about his discovery of why rainbows reflect the colorful prism they do. He created the *law of cooling*, which has played an important role centuries later in everything from nuclear safety to space exploration. He even went on to play a pivotal role in the British Parliament, helping to enact The Bill of Rights, which limited the power of the monarchy and laid out the rights of Parliament, as well as certain individual rights. His contributions were so vast he would be knighted in 1705 by Queen Anne.

But one of the top accomplishments that goes unnoticed and uncredited was Newton's commitment to stillness and solitude. Without creating the time and space to be still daily, one of the most brilliant thinkers in our world's history would have never been able to accomplish what he did.

Newton was asked later in his life how he worked out gravity. His response was "by thinking on it continually."

FLIP THE SCRIPT

You wake up today in Paris, France, with big plans to see the Eiffel Tower and experience one of the world's greatest monuments.

As you sit at the dining table of your hotel room, you sip your French press coffee, take a couple of bites from the fresh pâtisserie, and excitedly get up to head out for the day. Your hotel is at the top of Montmartre, the highest hill in Paris. Excited to see the entire landscape of one of the most beautiful cities in the world, you begin walking down the road in search of a tourist telescope.

Why can't you find one? Every major tourist city you have ever been to is flooded with telescopes and "selfie-worthy" panoramic view locations. How could Paris not have any?

Frustrated, you decide to walk down the hill and visit the Eiffel Tower. You search Eiffel Tower on your Google Maps, but it doesn't come up. Interesting. It must be the spotty phone service. You retreat to your hotel so the concierge can call a taxi to take you there. Surely, they will know the way.

But when you alert the concierge gentleman of your desired destination, his face displays a confusion that isn't just typical French annoyance for tourists.

"Eiffel what?" he asks.

Is this some sick joke? Is this Frenchman playing a cruel prank on you for the entertainment of the hotel staff?

"The Eiffel Tower," you repeat, this time with a "don't mess with me again" tone to your voice.

"I'm sorry, monsieur, I don't know where that is," the concierge says, convinced he is telling you the truth.

Confused and irritated, you go to your room. You remember you had packed a personal telescope to view Paris's breathtaking landscape from your 25th-floor balcony suite. Surely you can just take it to the rooftop and find the Eiffel Tower yourself. You rummage through your bag, but can't seem to find the telescope. Where did you put it? There's no way you could have misplaced it, could you?

You have waited all these years to visit Paris and lay your eyes on the majestic Eiffel Tower. And now, you could not find it on foot, correctly describe it to the French concierge worker, or even find a telescope to view it with.

Turns out, in this reality, Isaac Newton had decided not to step into solitude. He chose the path of trying to juggle everything all at once and allowed any shiny object within eyesight to steal his attention. He never achieved the world-changing feats that sealed his name in the history books.

And because he didn't, the Eiffel Tower was never created. Calculus is the driving force behind structural engineering, and without it, great accomplishments like building the Eiffel Tower are not possible.

Isaac Newton never put his touch on the telescope to eliminate chromatic aberration, which enables even the common person to see clearly for miles.

Remember this, you will never be able to achieve your destiny if you are too busy being consumed by the *noise of the world*. You need space, you need time to think, to create, to be free from notifications and random distractions.

Without time spent free of distractions, you will continue to be a prisoner of the world. Noise becomes your comfort. Stillness becomes your personal hell. When have you ever woken up and said, "Today I want as many *extreme agitations of the mind and emotions* as I can possibly get?

I hope the answer is never.

Don't put this book down and check your phone. Keep going and learn how to overcome distractions. Instead of battling the opponent: recruit the opponent to your team!

Tools to Overcome The Distraction

Did you ever have a pet goldfish? They always seem to dart this way and that way, never really able to focus on their directive path. Notoriously, the goldfish is known for its nine-second attention span. In 2015, Microsoft reported that the human attention span is actually one second *less* than a goldfish's. Eight seconds!

The only issue is, Microsoft was wrong. About goldfish, not humans. More recent research has shown that, contrary to popular belief and falsified reputation, the goldfish exhibits focused memory patterns for up to five months. The human being, not so much.

According to a study done by the University of San Diego in collaboration with Oxford University, employees generally spend 28% of their time dealing with distractions and unnecessary interruptions. The average worker wastes 60 hours every month due to workplace distractions. This is further exacerbated when 80% of interruptions at work are considered trivial.

Distractions are only going to increase. The question is, are you going to allow them to distract you from living the fulfilled life you have been searching for?

You know *why* you are one of the distracted; now it's time for me to show you how to conquer this archetype.

The Distraction Advantage

We are often told we should *avoid* distractions. And as great as that might sound in theory, it's much easier said than done. But what if there was a way to have your cake and eat it, too? And not only eat your cake but also have your cake work for you—and get you in better shape? Okay, that last part of the analogy might seem like a pipe dream, but when it comes to conquering distractions, it's not far off.

As of 2022, according to a study done by Reviews.org, the average American spends 2 hours and 54 minutes on their phone per day. That adds up to nearly a month and a half of an entire year!

71% of people say they check their phones within the first ten minutes of waking up.

53% say they have never gone 24 hours without checking their phone.

45% say their phone is their most valuable possession.

What?! Have we become completely controlled by our phones? The short answer: yes. The long answer: yes, we have.

Our phones are just one of the many distractions we have vying for our precious energy and attention. How do we get out of the quicksand of distractions we are slowly sinking into?

We use them to our advantage. Yep, flip the script and use distractions as the secret ace up your sleeve.

What if when you use social media, you do so only to post positive or meaningful messages that could help people instead of "death scrolling" for hours? Aside from work, what if you set the precedent that you will only respond to text messages and emails twice per day in 20-minute blocks in the morning and the evening? What if you set a limit to the number of streaming shows you watched per evening as a "one per night" decompressing treat? What if instead of looking at your kids as distractions to your weight loss goals, you exercise with your kids as a family activity? Remember, the best lessons are not taught, they are *caught*.

Distractions are all around us if we want them to be. But so are ample opportunities to take advantage of what others have deemed to be distractions. You can also build in your distractions. If that sounds counterproductive, good. It should.

If we allow ourselves intentional times of distraction throughout the day, we won't randomly indulge and won't sacrifice our productivity. We know distractions are going to happen. When we control them by dictating when and how long they occur, we regain the upper hand in the *distraction tug of war*.

This is known as the Pomodoro Technique (for a visual of the Pomodoro Technique, please visit www.DavidNurse.com). First, pick a task. Next, set a timer for 25 minutes. There are no other web browsers open, no notifications popping up anywhere, you are locked in for 25 minutes.

When the timer goes off, allow yourself five minutes of free time. Entertain any activity you want. It does not have to be task-oriented; it can even be your *favorite* distraction. My personal favorite is playing fetch with my puppy.

Once the five-minute timer goes off, you are back at it for another 25 minutes of undistracted work on your task. After four complete Pomodoro Technique cycles (two hours total) take a 15–30 min break. Then repeat another four cycles.

Two complete cycles per day will suffice, no more than three or your overall energy output will begin to produce diminishing returns.

Action step for today: Take a piece of paper and draw a line down the middle of the sheet. On the left side, list out all the "distractions" in your life.

On the right side of the paper, jot down all the names of the most important people in your life to spend time with and each thing you want to accomplish this year.

Now, draw a line, or as I call them *bridges*, to connect the distractions on the left with the names/goals written on the right and how they can link together.

Here's an example:

Distraction: Hour commute to and from work

Goal: To read 50 books this year.

Distraction Advantage: Bridge these two together and listen to the audiobook version on your commute.

Here's another example:

Distraction: I have three kids, how can I ever find time to exercise?

Goal: To lose 10 pounds and get back into shape

Distraction Advantage: Bridge these two together by playing ultimate frisbee with your kids at the park. Or, do a pushup challenge with your kids. Or, ride bikes through the countryside as a family. Or, do a free daily YouTube video dance class together. Or, easiest of all, go on a family walk! Teach your kids the importance of exercise, make family traditions and memories, and get your butt back into shape!

Now create your own Distraction Advantage list:

1. Write down a distraction that monopolizes your time and stresses you out.

2. Write down a goal (the thing you'd like to achieve but feel you can't due to your specific distraction).

3. Bridge the two together and recruit the distraction to your team!

The Daily Hawaiian Airline Flight Mentality

Do you remember the days when airplanes didn't have Wi-Fi? Oh, the peace. Even if you were crunched in a middle seat between Helga and Hans, you were still free. Free from the feeling you had to be *connected* to the world.

And then in 2003, Lufthansa decided it would be a good idea to offer Wi-Fi on their flights. *Uhhhh*. It's never been the same since.

We feel *anxious* if we are "out of the know."

- "Oh, you don't know who won the London Marathon? How dare you!"

- "Miss out on responding to the meme in the group chat? Catch up, bro."

- "Did you learn about the latest celebrity breakup two hours behind everyone else? Who are you?"

- "You haven't posted an inspiring quote since yesterday? Are you ill?"

You laugh at these examples, but it is all too real. Our society has normalized being "always in the know" to the point that we feel it is a *need*.

Nick Fitz, the senior behavioral researcher at Duke University's Center for Advanced Hindsight, conducted a study that found the average person gets 65–80 notifications on their phone daily. As we know, it can take the human mind 25 minutes to get back into the zone after checking just one notification (i.e., distraction).

So let's do some math to prove a point. Let's say you are the lucky few who has the low end of the notification average: 65. So, $65 \times 25 = 1,625$ minutes, or slightly over 27 hours. That is more than one day itself!!! The entire day distracted with no sleep?!

But it doesn't have to be this way. We don't have to let what Lufthansa started seep into our time and our lives.

Action step for today: Select a time during the day when you are going to hop on board the *Hawaiian airline flight* and put your phone on airplane mode. I use Hawaii, as I have joked with my wife that I would love to commute daily back and forth from Hawaii so I could get five hours of uninterrupted time when no one expects me to respond to them.

Start small with 30 minutes. You'll quickly discover the world continues to spin—even if you don't reply to every email and text message right away—and you'll feel more comfortable gradually increasing your "airplane mode" minutes.

Put the Hawaiian airplane flight time down in your calendar as an **important meeting** so you don't feel tempted to cancel on yourself.

YOUR ACTION ANIMAL: THE OWL

Often considered one of the wisest in the animal kingdom, the owl is your action animal if you are one of The Distracted. The owl has extraordinary night vision and far-sightedness, allowing them to spot prey miles away in the pitch black, dead of night. Their binocular vision permits extreme focus on their prey, with both eyes, for hours on end.

The owl is also able to rotate its head 270 degrees without making a sound or moving any other area of its body. When it comes to being locked in, focused, and remaining in complete solitude, the wise owl is the best in the business. It also has the uncanny ability to fly silently, allowing it to swoop down on its prey without making a peep.

Source: AnastasiaOsipova/Adobe Stock

The owl has incredible hearing, too. Thanks to its non-symmetrical ears, it can hear sounds sooner than the majority of other animals and almost always before its prey. It is a little-known fact that the eyes of an owl are not like human beings' eyes; Instead of eyeballs, it has eye tubes or cylinders; these rod-shaped eyes do not move in their sockets as eyeballs do. So instead, an owl has to move its body or head to look around. Not only does it give the owl the great ability to judge the height, weight, and distance of its prey, but also the ability to be unshakeable to distractions.

You are an owl. You have the ability to lock in and focus on what's most important: your prey (i.e., the task at hand). Don't buy the lies the world continues to spew, that "you must be doing 11 things all at once to be important; you must keep up with everyone around you; you must constantly be up to speed on every news headline within a 12,392-mile radius."

No. You don't. You are the owl; focus on what's most important. Distractions are for the birds. (The other birds, that is.)

"We build too many walls, and not enough bridges."
—Sir Isaac Newton

CHAPTER 9

The Underestimater

MEET JOHN OSTEEN

The sun was hot enough to fry an egg on the sidewalk. Classic Paris, Texas, John thought, as he finished up a grueling day's work on his family's cotton field. "Johnny boy, dinner time!" his mother bellowed from the front porch. Having recently dropped out of high school, John worked two jobs to help his family make ends meet: working in town at the local movie theater and picking cotton on the family farm.

"Ma, I'm famished. What's for dinner?" John implored as he plopped down at the table.

"Sorry, darlin'. Ain't no point gettin' your hopes up. I'm afraid it's more of the same," his mother conceded as she placed a bowl of lumpy pea soup in front of him.

"I sure miss your creamed chicken and homemade biscuits," John mumbled as he stared at the thick soup and sad stack of Ritz crackers.

The year was 1939, and like most families throughout the United States, the Osteens suffered the ramifications of the Great Depression. "I miss makin' it myself, sugar. But we'll get to have it again soon enough, won't we, Jack?" John's mother queried his father.

"As long as the boy keeps workin' his butt off on the farm," his dad chimed from the head of the table.

"I know, Pa, I will," John promised faintly.

The Great Depression had ripped through the United States, and families had to be *all hands on deck* just to provide enough food to put on the dinner table. John was used to waking up in the morning to an empty fridge and hearing his mother anxiously report there was nothing left to eat. Sometimes, his family would stand in bread lines for hours on end, just waiting for their portion of free food.

The only thing keeping them afloat—barely—was the family farm. John's parents, Willis "Jack" and Ellen, came from modest upbringings. Neither attended college and, instead, carried on the family farming tradition.

Why would John disrupt the norm? There was no reason to. His entire life was planned out in front of him. Plus, his father was a good man, kind-hearted, and well-respected throughout the community. John looked up to his father. Following in his footsteps wouldn't be the worst thing.

Like most of the 17-year-old boys in Paris, Texas, John lived for the weekends. Work hard through the week; enjoy the weekends at the dance hall with his friends. "I'm heading out, Ma," John announced after shoveling down his last mouthful of soup.

That evening at the dance hall, it was a routine Friday night. John and his buddies had a good time, but as the responsible young adult John was, he knew it was time to head back to the farm before he had one too many.

A cloudy velvet sky stretched over the highway that night, providing little light for the path ahead. As John's truck traveled through the black abyss, his mind began to wander. "What is the meaning of this life I'm living?" he thought to himself. "Was I put here to pick cotton and run a farm and drink beers on the weekend my entire life? There has to be more, right?" he questioned aloud.

"What happens when I die?"

"Am I living a life of purpose?"

These questions and more began to overtake John's mind—thoughts he had never entertained before. "Don't be foolish. I'm a farmer from Paris, Texas. That's who I was made to be, and that's all I'll ever be," John finally convinced himself, gripping the wheel a little tighter now.

Suddenly, a faint light appeared ahead like a beacon in the night. The first vehicle he'd seen for miles. John found himself transfixed by the approaching headlights as they grew brighter and brighter until his entire face was aglow, momentarily blinding him. A single name came to mind: Sam.

WHOOSH! The vehicle zipped past, taking every ounce of light with it. John stared ahead, puzzled: "Sam?"

As John lay awake in bed that night, his internal wrestling match didn't subside. He couldn't shake the thought that there was more to life than just being a cotton farmer. And what was this business about "Sam?" he thought. The only Sam he knew was from his high school. Sam Matin.

John always found Sam to be a little odd and often kept his distance from him. Most of John's buddies referred to Sam as the "Jesus freak." If he wasn't talking about Jesus in his school presentations, you could usually find him telling kids at lunch how "Jesus is the Way." It wasn't that John didn't like Sam, he just didn't *get* him. Didn't understand. "What if Sam was right?" John thought now. "What if all of this 'the Way' stuff Sam rambled on about was true? What if there was a better way?"

John rolled out of bed the next morning with Sam still on his mind. He had been relieved of his cotton-picking duties for the weekend. So, with a full day ahead of him and no chores in sight, John came up with a new plan. He headed to Sam's house.

"John?" Sam questioned with a cocked brow as he answered the door. He was just as confused to see John on his doorstep as John was to be there.

"I have a few questions and I didn't know where else to go," John explained.

"Oh, okay, uh sure, come on in," Sam offered as he held the door for John.

"You know how you always goin' on about Jesus being 'the Way'? What's that all about anyway? What does it even mean? Cause I had a whole bunch of crazy thoughts and feelings tugging at my heart last night on the drive home from the dance hall. Questions and things about life and where you go when you die and my life's purpose and—"

"Whoa, slow down, John, one at a time," Sam interjected. "Why don't you start from the beginning, huh? How's that sound?" Sam asked warmly. Something about his tone calmed John's racing heart. He drew in a breath and started from the beginning.

Sam and John talked for hours, going back and forth on questions involving the meaning of life and who this *Jesus* guy was. Suddenly, everything about John's life felt meaningless. His eyes were opened and by the end of the conversation, John knew what he had to do. He wanted to be a pastor and share the hope that Sam shared with him. He knew it wouldn't be easy, but something about it felt right. He wasn't meant to live out his entire life picking cotton, stuck in poverty. He had a new purpose.

The only problem was *that* life was the only life he had ever known. It was the life his parents and their parents had known, too. What made him any different from them? Suddenly, his mind was flooded with doubt. "I didn't even finish high school. Who am I to be a pastor? How would I even start?" he thought as he slipped back into his truck.

As he drove home, his hesitations grew louder, "I don't even know the Bible, let alone know how to teach it to others. I'm just John Osteen from nowhere Paris, Texas. Who am I to do anything great?"

John pulled up to the family home. Did he really have the courage to stroll through that door, pack his bags, and set off on a journey into the unknown? Did he really feel a call from God? Should he be more *realistic*? More humble in his pursuits? Paris, Texas, was all he knew. It was all anyone he knew ever knew.

As his hand hovered over the doorknob, John felt his heart thumping faster in his chest. He had a decision to make: listen to his head or follow his heart.

THE CRUX

Does John Osteen decide to accept that he is made for more and leave all he has ever known in Paris, Texas, in pursuit of what his heart is pulling him toward? Or does he settle and continue to live the life he has always known, accepting that great things are for other people?

Raise your hand if you love a great underdog story.

My hand just skyrocketed to the ceiling! Did yours? *Rocky*, *Rudy*, *The Miracle on Ice*, even *Legally Blonde* for that matter . . . the list goes on and on. We all love the story of an underdog for one reason—we can see ourselves in that character.

You are an underdog. I am an underdog. But why is it that when we watch these movies or read these incredible stories of an underdog that overcomes great odds, we think "Well, must be nice"?

Why do you underestimate your underdog power? It's like having the opportunity to play in the hot seat on *Who Wants to Be a Millionaire*, but then tapping out before they even ask the first question. You don't even give yourself a shot.

The greatest underdog of all was David. (Not me, but I'll take the comparison if you want to make it.) Here is an undersized, naive sheepherder who had never done anything noteworthy in his life, yet King Saul asks to speak with him. No one else wants to fight an 8-foot giant (think The Rock, but even bigger) and Saul asks David if he is up for the task. It's obviously a no-brainer; there's no way anybody would even think about fighting someone who is twice his size and a bona fide *killer*, right? Wrong.

David knew he was an underdog, and he knew what everyone else was saying about him. Too small, no experience, painfully underqualified. But what David also knew was that he had an *x*-factor: belief in himself.

The only reason you don't accomplish a David-sized takedown is because you *underestimate* yourself.

David stepped onto the battlefield and stared down the possibility of failure, humiliation, and for him, death. He picked up his slingshot and, without hesitation, took his best shot; it hit the massive Goliath right between the eyes, dropping him cold on the battlefield.

David finished the job, and the rest is history. He went on to become one of the greatest kings ever known to man. Not bad for an underdog sheepherder.

The Brain

Underestimating is derived from low self-esteem. The main chemical in the brain responsible for self-esteem is serotonin; it is associated with mood stabilization. According to a study performed by the Cleveland Clinic in 2021, low serotonin levels are directly linked with low self-esteem and depression. Ninety percent of the serotonin in your body is found in the lining of your gastrointestinal tract. It reaches the brain through blood circulation. This is one of the many reasons your gut is referred to as your *second brain*. Serotonin cannot be made by your body on its own; it is obtained from the foods you eat, specifically healthy fats. So, think again before you reach for another bag of processed chips, and instead make the switch to a handful of nuts and seeds, or cook up a hearty omelet consisting of eggs, cheese, salmon, and chicken.

The other key hormone that plays a crucial role in your ability to overcome the *underestimater* mindset is dopamine. Dopamine is the "feel-good" hormone. It is the reward center that gives you the sense of pleasure. According to the same 2021 study, low levels of dopamine are also directly linked to low self-esteem and depression. The foods known to improve dopamine are rich in magnesium and tyrosine, such as chicken, almonds, apples, avocados, bananas, beets, chocolate (yes, chocolate), green leafy vegetables, green tea, lima beans, oatmeal, oranges, peas, sesame and pumpkin seeds, tomatoes, and turmeric.

Another important player in regulating self-esteem is what is known as *white matter*. A 2014 Dartmouth study reported that the stronger the white matter connection between the medial cortex and the ventral striatum, the higher the self-esteem of the individual.

White matter—the nerves responsible for the information highway that is your brain—is made up of a large network of nerve fibers that allow for the exchange of information and communication between the different areas of your brain. The best ingredient to grow white matter, once again, comes from what you eat. Healthy fats such as eggs, avocados, coconut, grass-fed beef, and fresh-caught fatty fish are some of the best white matter brain foods. I'm not trying to turn this into a cookbook, but I want you to see why this is important for boosting self-esteem.

So now that we know what chemically (internally) affects white matter, let's look at what externally affects it. The short answer: feedback.

Think of it like this: white matter is like a dog that is encouraged for its actions. Its tail lifts upwards and wags. On the flipside, when the dog is discouraged from doing something, its tail shrinks between its legs. The same thing applies to humans and white matter. The growth of white matter changes based on feedback from other people.

You might be thinking, "Isn't this a lot like the first chapter: *fear of other people's opinions?*"

No. Here's what makes all the difference. Underestimaters are not *not* taking action because they fear what other people think; their motives don't derive from their need to secure the validation of others. Underestimaters are not scared of what others think, they just *believe* what others think. They limit themselves to a box that is constructed from the feedback of other people.

It's not a matter of *what will people think if I do this*, it's a matter of *what do people think I can do*.

If your parents once said that the odds of you ever becoming a lawyer were slim to none, your white matter shrank. Your brain believes you won't become a lawyer; your self-esteem for accomplishing great things lowers. If your guidance counselor said your dream college rarely, if ever, accepts anyone like you, white matter shrinks. Your brain believes you are not *college material*. If the stylist at a clothing store mentioned the outfit you tried on isn't flattering to your body type, white matter shrinks. Every time you look in the mirror from there on out your brain sees an unflattering reflection staring back. If your co-worker discounts an exciting idea you present in the boardroom, white matter shrinks. Your brain no longer believes your ideas are smart enough to express.

But feedback goes both ways. Most people rely on hearing positive feedback from others and need it before they believe they can accomplish doing something. In her study "Forming Global Estimates of Self-performance from Local Confidence," Dr. Marion Rouault states, "We found that people performed the tasks equally well in the presence and absence of feedback—however, they clearly underestimated their ability when positive feedback was withheld."

Interesting. They underestimated themselves because they are reliant on having someone tell them they are capable of more.

Before I break that down even further, let's take a look at the three *self* terms that are important to understand.

- *Self-esteem:* your ability to appreciate and value yourself
- *Self-confidence:* your belief in yourself and your abilities
- *Self-efficacy:* your belief in your capacity to act alone in the ways necessary to reach specific goals

To accomplish self-efficacy, you must have both self-esteem and self-confidence. Unfortunately, and fortunately, these are inhibited by both the presence and lack of feedback.

If you don't have anybody to provide negative feedback in regard to your value or abilities as a human being, then you will internally have more self-esteem and self-confidence. But on the flipside, if you don't have anybody to provide encouraging or positive feedback in regard to your values or abilities, then you will underestimate yourself and will not be inclined to accomplish what you are capable of.

In other words, your self-esteem and self-confidence don't accurately reflect your abilities. The ideal situation for achieving self-efficacy is to become blind to the limiting views other people have about you, appreciate the uplifting views other people have about you, and rely mainly on an intentionally crafted view of yourself that is humble, yet aspiring. One that you don't allow any outside forces to detract from.

We underestimate ourselves because our self-esteem and self-confidence have been tainted over the years. When this happens, we no longer have self-efficacy. Remember, the *underestimater* doesn't care what others think about them, they *believe* what others think about them is true.

There is one more piece of the puzzle that makes all the difference: the future.

According to research using extensive brain imagery, visualization works because neurons in our brains interpret imagery as equivalent to a real-life action. When you visualize an act, the brain creates a connection that tells your neurons to perform the action.

This creates a new neural pathway priming your body to act in a way consistent with the way you visualize it to be. All of this occurs without actually performing the physical activity but both achieve similar results.

In summary, if you eat the right foods to increase serotonin and dopamine, if you filter feedback the correct way to increase self-efficacy, and if you train your brain to visualize the future version of yourself you want to become, you have the ultimate trifecta to combat and overcome the *underestimater*.

The Heart

Now imagine for a second, as morbid as it might sound, that you are on your deathbed breathing in your final gulps of air. Your mind ruminates on the things you "wish you would have done." Now if you are in the same mindset as the majority of people, your top deathbed regrets are as follows:

- I wish I'd had the courage to live a life true to myself.

- I wish I had taken more risks.

- I wish I had lived my dream.

Wow. Not thoughts of wanting more money, plush comforts, an easier upbringing, exotic travels, nope, none of that. *More courage to be true to myself. More courage to take risks and live out my dream.* Sounds like these people highly underestimated their ability to take action in these areas. They needed courage, but underestimating yourself is the diametric opposite of courage.

According to a survey conducted by OnePoll on behalf of Little Passports, one in six US adults have never left their home state. Talk about taking the phrase "there's no place like home" a little too seriously. Out of the survey participants who have traveled, many stated how formative traveling during childhood was for them. If they expanded their horizons at a young age by either (1) being introduced to travel firsthand or (2) being told they would one day travel, their heart felt courageous enough to leave home when they became adults. Out of those who never left, many underestimated their ability and desire to do so. It's easy to get stuck in the comforts and confinements if your heart was never given the chance to feel the thrill of going beyond.

On the encouraging flipside, 80% of millionaires in America are first-generation millionaires, aka "the ones who didn't *underestimate* themselves." A lot of them credit involving their heart in the process by practicing *dream-setting*. Instead of looking at that life and thinking "How could I ever accomplish something that monumental," they get excited and invest their emotions by imagining the future life they long for. Their heart feels as if they are already the version of themselves who has grown and accomplished their dreams.

We all have a mountain towering directly ahead of us—and will have mountains our entire lives. You can either look at the daunting mountain ahead and say, "How am I ever going to get to the top of it?" Or you can look at that same mountain and say, "This is going to be an exhilarating adventure to get to the top, and once I'm there I'll have a great story to tell."

Your under-*estimation* is exactly that, your own *estimation*.

Estimation is a powerful term, ultimately meaning "Do you believe you deserve to do *great* things in your life, or do you believe those *great* things are for someone else?"

Enter *memetics theory*. Once our basic needs are met, human beings move into a realm of *desire*. This desire is not led by hormones but instead is non-instinctual and purely social. Our lives now become overshadowed by the desire to have what others have or be who others are.

Renè Girard first mainstreamed the memetics theory after realizing the girl he had just broken up with was dating someone else. The rejection and the knowledge that *another man* had her heart only intensified Renè's desire for his former flame and decreased his belief he deserved her. Realizing he couldn't have her made him want her more but also made him believe he wasn't good enough to deserve her.

When you scroll through social media, have ever you thought, "Wow, I wish I was like _____ [fill in the blank] because they are living a much more fulfilling life and making a real impact. But I can't do that." Have you ever looked at _____, who is doing your dream job, and thought, "If only I could do that, but I'm not qualified"? Or have you ever aspired to be that happy couple you know, _____, and thought "I wish my marriage was as wonderful and loving as theirs, but I'm not capable or worthy of it"?

Guess what? The answer to all of these questions is: you can. But only if you follow your heart and stop underestimating yourself.

What Actually Happened to John Osteen?

As John Osteen stood in the dusty doorway of his Texas farmhouse, sweat dripping from his brow, his calling became clear; he was meant to share the Word of God. But it was a call outside his norm—it didn't involve picking cotton—and he was unsure of his ability to do it.

"A preacher? College? Leaving the farm?" He could already hear the barrage of questions he'd have to defend from his family and friends.

But John anchored himself on the frayed welcome mat, shoulders tall, boots firmly planted. His decision was made. He'd turn that handle, march right on inside, deflect their doubts—including his own—and take action.

And that's exactly what he did. John left the farm to get his bachelor's degree (something no one in his family had done before) from John Brown University and went on to get his master's from Northern Baptist Seminary.

Acting on the thing he felt God was calling him to do, John made it his mission to share the Word of God anywhere and everywhere he could, and he refused to let self-doubt stop him. Throughout college, he'd routinely hitchhike to neighboring towns to preach at their church. Where there was a will, there was a way, and John always found a way.

Despite the hurdles, John refused to let stats on how many churches fail, or any daunting challenges deter him. He was all in.

A few years later, John found himself plagued with self-doubt once again after his first wife filed for divorce. He'd just entered full-time ministry and a new wave of insecurity was begging to take hold. Here he was, finally pastoring, but how could he continue knowing his marriage had failed? In that day and age, divorce was a social disqualifier for a pastor. He contemplated whether he could continue preaching, or if he should throw in the towel because it was an unrealistic pursuit. How could someone so broken speak into the lives of so many?

But John chose to silence the lies his mind hurled at him about not being good enough. He ignored what everyone else thought of him, and continued to do what he felt called to do. Eventually, he went on to marry Dolores "Dodie" Pilgrim, and she motivated him to keep believing in himself. She recognized his gift for preaching and championed his every effort. This encouraged John to become the head pastor at Hibbard Memorial Baptist Church in Houston, Texas.

His church was growing, his family was thriving, and then out of the clear blue, life punched John straight in the throat. A major health issue arose in their family and John was devastated. Trying to make sense of it, he retreated to a hotel room in solitude searching for answers in the Bible. As he read over verses he'd read hundreds of times before, a specific one jumped out to him in a new way—as a message of hope and freedom. An interpretation he'd never been taught in church before.

But who was he, the pastor of an average little church who came from nothing and had no grandiose credentials, to share such a powerful message of prosperity?

Deep down, John knew that ignoring this calling would mean he was giving into the underestimations people tried to label on him his whole life. He refused to fall back into the mindset that he wasn't good enough. This message was too important. His mission was clear.

That next Sunday John stepped up to the pulpit to preach the message of hope he felt called to share. But this message wasn't welcomed with open arms, quite the opposite. The people of Hibbard Memorial Baptist disagreed and rejected him, ultimately asking John to step down and cease pastoring the church.

But instead of rolling over, John took action. He embraced being the underdog. He decided to start his own church, which he called Lakewood. Its first service was held in a small, grubby abandoned feed store in Northeast Houston. All of six people showed up for the first service. But the miracle was just beginning.

John went on to grow Lakewood Church to more than 15,000 members, even hosting a weekly TV program that reached millions in the US and many other countries throughout the world. The groundwork he laid and the legacy he left has only continued to grow. What started in an abandoned feed store with only six people, is now held in the former Houston Compaq Center and home to 50,000 members. Today, Lakewood Church provides hope to over 200 million households worldwide each week.

As the *underestimater*, you often doubt whether the choices you make are realistic. You always cling to the things that disqualify you out of fear that you are not good enough. And if you tell yourself you can't do something, and you believe you can't, then guess what—you definitely won't. But you don't have to spend your life trapped in the box others limit you to. Drown out the noise and have faith you can accomplish more than you can even imagine. The only thing that disqualifies you is yourself. Don't let *you* stand in the way of living the life you want.

FLIP THE SCRIPT

You wake up this morning and immediately pull the covers back up and over your head.

You're not feeling it.

Another day to *get through*.

Sure, you have ambition. You have goals bigger than the present life situation you are currently in.

But how could *you* achieve them? Little ole you. If only you had something to inspire your soul. You need it, you can feel it.

You remember hearing multiple times from your coworkers about a TV show and corresponding podcast that speaks of hope, freedom, and encouragement.

What was it called??

"The Joel Osteen Show," that's right.

"What could it hurt?" you think out loud between sips of your coffee.

You turn on the TV guide as you simultaneously reach for an outfit to wear for the day.

You have a big meeting at the office *and* a client call you have been stressing about for days.

"If I don't nail this call, I could lose everything I've worked for," you think as you scroll through the channel guide.

Nothing.

Well, maybe it's just a radio show. You definitely remember they said he has his own radio station.

You turn on Sirus XM radio and push "scan" as you watch the different radio show names change every three seconds until you go through them all.

Still nothing.

Where is this *show of hope?*

You could really use it today, and of course today of all days you can't find it. Just your luck.

You look at your watch and notice you are already running behind schedule. The already heightened stress you are feeling jumps up another notch on the scale. You scurry out the door and drive to the office with more doubt and self-discouragement than you had woken up with. "I just hope I *get through* this day," you think as you shut your car door and head toward the office building looming ahead of you like a daunting mountain.

There is no "Joel Osteen Show" or radio program. There isn't even a church where he pastors. There aren't any messages by him about hope, freedom, and encouragement.

John Osteen, Joel's father, never took the chance. Instead of acting on the call God had placed on his heart during that fateful drive back in Paris, Texas, John decided to believe he wasn't qualified to do anything greater than the path he was already on. He stuck to the safe route and believed his choices didn't make a difference.

But the choices we downplay as only affecting *ourselves* in the moment have the capacity and power to have a ripple effect on millions of people for generations to come.

Because John Osteen underestimated himself, he never left the farm. He never made an impact with his messages of hope, healing, and freedom.

Don't sit on the bench your whole life because you think making a difference is *unattainable* for you. Don't take the route of least resistance when the rocky road that leads to generational abundance is around the corner. The next time you count yourself out, understand that you are also counting out your kids, their kids, their kid's kids, and on and on.

Why not be the one who changes the trajectory of your family's legacy and possibly the world? John Osteen did it. So can you.

TOOLS TO OVERCOME THE UNDERESTIMATER

Have you ever walked into a movie theater expecting the movie to be average at best, but then walked out after the show raving about it?

This is the benefit of being underestimated. There are no high expectations of what you can bring to the table, and the element of surprise you are able to deliver catches people off guard and makes them pay attention.

All this to say, when someone underestimates you, what they're really doing is gifting you with the opportunity to surpass their wildest expectations. Being underestimated gives you the freedom to find your own way and allows you to take risks others won't.

You know *why* you are the underestimater; now it's time for me to show you how to conquer this archetype.

Endowment Effect of Your Future Life

The endowment effect is an emotional bias that causes a person to value an object they own much more than its market value. This added personal value is usually the result of a strong emotional tie.

Think of the most beloved stuffed animal from your childhood. If you're lucky enough to still own it today, the value is extremely high to you, yet you would probably be lucky to get even 50 cents if you tried to sell it now based on its actual market value.

Now the tool I want you to implement into your life is the *endowment effect* of your future, which requires you to place an extremely high value on the person you are going to become.

Your future is worth more to you than that teddy bear you once thought was priceless. Sure, keep the teddy bear if you would like, but from now on your future is the highest valued object you own.

According to behavioral economists, irrational behavior from the endowment effect often stems from a blinding cognitive bias: loss aversion. Humans hate experiencing a loss about twice as much as they enjoy experiencing a gain. You don't want to lose what you already have. So, if you consider your future as something you already have, you will do anything it takes not to lose it. The more you can envision who your future self is going to be, the more difficult it will become to let that future self go (i.e., give up on your dreams).

The endowment effect makes you feel psychological ownership over a product, which increases your will to spend more on it. So if you replace the word "product" in the former sentence with "your future," wouldn't that mean you'd be more willing to invest (time and finances) in your future self?

Your future exists, it will happen, there is no doubt about that.

But it won't happen the way you want it to unless you hold on to your future now like it's your favorite childhood teddy bear.

Do this today: Choose someone you admire and look up to. Pick someone who has accomplished great things, similar to what you aspire to accomplish. Take a piece of paper or your journal and then do the following:

1. Write the person's name followed by one of their major achievements you look up to.

    Example: James Clear wrote one of the best-selling motivational books in the past 20 years.

2. Write the person's name followed by one thing about their character that stands out to you.

    Example: James Clear is a very humble human being.

3. Write the person's name followed by a big moment in their life that they overcame.

   Example: James Clear refused to allow a life-changing setback in high school to dictate his future.

4. Write the person's name followed by something positive about them that really stands out to you.

   Example: James Clear consistently provides thought-provoking content.

5. Write the person's name followed by why they are the person you chose.

   Example: James Clear decided to become a writer, has stayed true to his habits, and accomplishes what he sets his mind to, regardless of his pedigree.

Now, cross out (or erase if you can) that person's name from each statement. Fill in YOUR NAME where their name previously was.

What that person can do, *you* can do as well!

Keep this paper in the same spot you store valuable items. Refer to it anytime you feel yourself underestimate *you*.

Activate the endowment effect for your future!

Overexaggeration Training

In the athletic realm, the term *overspeed* is used by sprinters. Overspeed simply means the athlete increases the speed they run at during training. To boost their speed, they must either increase the length or frequency of their stride. Athletes have an anatomical limit to their stride length, so massive gains in their speed must come from increasing frequency. To increase the frequency of the turnover in the sprinters' legs, they step on a treadmill and crank up the speed past the point of their normal training speed.

The theory behind overspeed training is that once the mind registers that the legs can hit higher speeds, a new top speed is programmed into the mind.

The same concept is used in baseball and golf. The athletes will be given a heavier bat or club, swinging it as hard and as fast as they can. The more they use the weighted version, the lighter the normal version becomes to the mind.

When we apply *overspeeding* to our goals, they are known as *stretch goals*. Stretch goals will radically surpass any current capability or past performance. When setting these stretch goals, it's not necessarily about achieving them to full capacity. The point of this style of goal setting is to break free from the plateau of underestimating yourself.

Let's say, for example, you only think you can make $70,000 per year. That is the limit your mind has set for yourself, aka the plateau. Now, let's get a little crazy here and overestimate. This year your stretch goal is to make $400,000. Wow, how nice would that be?!

Now your mind is motivated to hit this stretch goal of $400,000, and that becomes your upper limit. It will be extremely difficult, and you will have to think of new ways to reach this goal that you didn't do in the past year.

Let's say you don't hit your new goal of $400,000. Should you be discouraged? Absolutely not! As long as you put in the work necessary to hit $400,000, you should be proud of *any* growth. More than likely you will land somewhere between the $70,000 you usually made and the *stretch goal* you set. Let's say you fell way short and landed on $150,000 for the year. You just failed your way to twice as much as you made the year before.

Overestimate what you can do and your mind will show you it can.

The will of the mind is the most powerful when you don't let it sit on a level plateau. Complacency is the killer of all innovation.

Be content, yes, but never complacent.

Do this today: Write down your goals for the year. Be as specific as possible with your goals. For example, here are a few of mine:

I want to take an entire month off to travel with my wife.

I want to start a side business to make passive income.

Now, here is where *overspeeding* comes into play. Next to the goals you have written I want you to stretch the goals and shoot for the moon. Here are the ones I wrote down but now with that adjustment:

I want to take an entire month off to travel with my wife and stay only in five-star resorts.

I want to start a side business that makes enough money that I could quit my day job if I choose to.

The point of this tool is to stretch your goals to levels where you will question, "Is it even possible?" When you embrace *overtraining* and shoot for the impossible, you are able to create the possible.

YOUR ACTION ANIMAL: THE NARWHAL

Often referred to as the *unicorn of the sea*, the narwhal is an elusive creature that has proven hard to be studied. You may know the narwhal by its one spiral tusk in the middle of its forehead. In actuality, this is a projecting tooth that can grow up to 9 meters long, Not previously considered to have any positive impact on the environment, the narwhal has been vastly overlooked outside of children's books and TV programs.

Until now.

The narwhal may be the reason society can stay ahead of the melting polar ice caps. Talk about carrying the weight of the world on your tusk!

NASA's Oceans Melting Greenland Project considers the nar-whal to be the lead oceanographer in their research of climate change in the melting Greenland ice sheet.

Source: dottedyeti/Adobe Stock

Eight percent of the world's freshwater is trapped under this sheet, and the once-solid block of ice is not nearly as solid as it once was. As the ice sheet continues to melt, water levels continue to rise throughout the world's oceans, endangering coastal cities worldwide.

Enter the narwhal. Researchers have attached a tracking device to narwhals, which helps to measure the temperature of the ice sheet every time they swim just below it.

Until this tracking research, it was very difficult for scientists to predict the rate at which the ice was melting and the rate at which water levels throughout the world would rise. But thanks to the once underestimated narwhal, oceanographers can now more accurately plan for how to counteract the melting of Greenland.

Just because people might not think you are capable of making a difference, doesn't mean you can't change the world just like our real-life unicorn of the sea, the narwhal.

They aren't the only elusive horned creature you share similarities with. Fantastical stories from our childhood have long assured us that no two unicorns are the same. Likewise, there is only one you on this entire planet. Think about that—8 billion people and only *one* you. Are you the one they've underestimated? Will you be the reason the world changes for the better?

Embrace your inner narwhal and find out.

"You cannot think negative thoughts and expect to live a positive life."

—John Osteen

CONCLUSION

For if anyone is a hearer of the word and not a doer, he is like a man who looks intently at his natural face in a mirror. For he looks at himself and goes away and at once forgets what he was like. But the one who looks into the perfect law, the law of liberty, and perseveres, being no hearer who forgets but a doer who acts, he will be blessed in his doing.

James 1:23–25

I'm not going to send you off on a positive, fuzzy note trying to convince you that you will "change the world." I do believe you can, but the pressure of that goal isn't something I want for you or anyone. I want you to finish this book and realize that you have a newfound awareness of your roadblocks and the tools to overcome them. You possess exactly what it takes to live a life of fulfillment. And just by doing that, you will have an impact on the world in ways you can't even imagine.

Martha Graham, Lewis Lattimer, Sybil Ludington, Wilma Rudolph, Isabel Briggs, Ward Piggy Lambert, James Harrison, Isaac Newton, and John Osteen didn't follow their hearts and define their purposes for the sole benefit of fame or being mentioned in a few history books. No, they were simply pursuing a life that fulfilled them. They made the decision to take action. Each started with baby steps and aimed to have an impact on the people around them first. They stayed committed to their dreams and refused to let anything or anyone hold them back. The crux moment in which they finally made the crucial decision to take action wasn't immediately followed by vigorous rounds of applause and congratulatory hugs. It was probably just the opposite. Many of them heard silence, maybe even crickets. At the time, they had no guarantee their decision would pay off. All they had was trust and faith. Trust in their commitment to take action and faith it would yield success. And that it certainly did.

Your name might never be known by millions of people. Truth is, 99.99% of us won't even be remembered 100 years from now. So why spend the only time you've got living in fear? Why not do what fulfills you? Why waste any more time stuck behind a roadblock when you know exactly how to move past it?

I hope you feel empowered to allow yourself to heal from what has been holding you back and give yourself permission to truly live. Happiness is what we seek, fulfillment is the key to happiness, and *taking action* is the vehicle that will get you there.

As we wrap up this book I hope you understand your journey is just beginning. I do believe your best days are in front of you and I hope you do, too. I hope you have been able to see yourself more clearly.

WHICH ACTION ARCHETYPE ARE YOU?

I'm sure you found yourself relating closer to one or two of the Action Archetypes. That's great; the awareness is very important. But the truth is, you are not just *one or two* of the archetypes, you are all of them. At some point in your life, you will experience every one of these Action Archetypes in different seasons of your life.

I know for a fact I have:

The Allodoxaphobic. I moved three times in high school and each time I feared what my new classmates would think of me.

The Burned. When I first began training NBA players, I worked with a high-profile player who promised to pay me after the season ended. All of our work together paid off for him and he had a great season; however, he completely stiffed me and didn't pay a dime.

The Inopportune. When I decided to become a motivational keynote speaker, I researched the ages of all the most successful speakers; they were all at least 20 years older than I was.

The Blamer. When I was young, I was promised by my doctor I would grow to be 6'6". When I only grew to 6'1", I blamed the doctor and my parents as the reason I never achieved my childhood dream of making the NBA.

The Test Believer. I've often been fearful of vulnerability when giving talks or interacting in the business world ever since reading the description of an Enneagram 7 with a wing of an 8. I fear the only way to effectively influence others is by using my exuberant energy and bold leadership.

The Perfectionist. When I was in middle school, I wanted to play the drums in my school's music recital. However, since I never had formal lessons, I told myself I would wait until I had years of practice before I signed up. I never signed up.

The Scarciest. In the past I have been jealous of others' success and seen other NBA trainers/coaches as competitors rather than people to collaborate with.

The Distracted. I have often felt like I have to get back to everyone who messages me or emails me within seconds of receiving it. This used to take me away from focused work and quality time with my wife.

The Underestimater. Before I wrote my first book, I strongly questioned whether I could even write a book, let alone become a best-selling author, due to the fact I didn't have the credentials to be a writer.

Your spouse, your children, your friends, your colleagues, the people you interact with on the street—every one of those people is an Action Archetype as well.

Think about how much of an advantage you have now that you have an in-depth understanding of all nine archetypes—an advantage in conversational interactions, in business meetings, in your personal relationships, in parenting, and in being a better *you*.

The greatest thing about taking action is that once you get over the hurdle of fear and accomplish your first dose of taking action, you won't want to stop. It's addicting, in a very healthy way. It won't be easy at first, but once you get the hang of it and you build the tools into your routine and mindset, then eventually taking action will feel second nature. It will become effortless for you. It will become freeing.

There is no good reason *not* to take action. As long as the action has a truly positive and pure motive behind it, then there will never be a wrong time to take action.

Now that you have all the tools that are necessary to overcome your hurdles and effectively take action, it is time to create your own story.

Remember Mad Libs? I want you to fill out the below Create Your Own Story "Mad Lib" with the goal of joy. Fill in each blank with the answers personal to you.

CREATE Your Own Story

My name is _____. The Action Archetype I most identify with is
        (full name)

_____. I live in the beautiful city of ___.
(name one or two archetypes from this book)   (city)

Every morning I wake up and start my morning off with _____.
                                                   (morning activity)

I have a gorgeous _____ whom I love deeply.
                    (significant other or family member)

I am gifted. I have a unique skill of being able to _____, which
                                              (special skill)

I have really developed. I'm also skilled at _____, in which I am
                                        (special skill)

continuing to develop. And although I haven't maximized this skill set

to its fullest quite yet, that's okay because I am and will continue to

work on it. It's a daily adventure of growth.

I struggle with letting go of _____ from my past.
(personal roadblock)

Even though I don't want to admit it, I know it's holding me back.

I don't quite feel worthy of success. _____ is something I am
(flaw/weakness)
insecure about.

It hurts; if everyone else knew this about me, that I have this black
eye, they would surely think differently of me. But it's a thing I make
sure to share with my _____
(mom, dad, sibling, friend, significant other, therapist, etc.)
named _____. I will continue to always trust and confide in them
(person's name)
no matter what. Thank God for that person!

I have had success in the past, actually, moments of really great
success. The time I _____ is a positive memory I will
(accomplishment or award)
never forget.

When I think about it, I have lived a good life. Not everything has
been perfect, but overall, I can't complain.

Even my childhood wasn't quite as bad as I once thought it was.
A great childhood memory of _____ comes to
(enjoyable activity, holiday, vacation, etc.)
mind. A smile comes to my face, and a sense of warm joy fills my heart.

That's neither here nor there, though; the real-life moment is on
me and the big opportunity I have is looming in the near future. I know

the person I want to become, and I know what it is going to take to get

there. _____ is something I can see myself doing, but I also know
(big opportunity)

that it's going to be a risk. There is no guarantee that it will work out,

or that the process will be easy either. I believe in myself, but I've been

hesitant to go all in because I fear _____. If only I could be
(fear holding you back)

more like _____. I know he/she would have no issue going
(person you look up to)

full force toward the decision I am faced with.

     I'll weigh the pros and cons.

     Some of the pros are _____, _____, and _____.
(positive) (positive)   (positive)

     But there are also cons that rear their ugly head like _____, _____
(negative) (nega-

___, and _____.
tive)   (negative)

     I think about what life could look like five years from now if I take

a risk and take action: _____.
(one to two sentences describing a life of fulfillment)

     I also think what life will be like if I don't go for it. If I stay in the

same exact spot I am currently in, I could miss out on: _____
(dreams and goals you

_____.
want to accomplish)

     I know the future I want, but the question is: Am I willing to do

what it takes to achieve that future?

I know that if I commit to beginning with the following tools from this book that speak to me the most: (1) _____, (2) _____
(tool from Chapter __)   (tool from
_____, and (3) _____, and practice them daily, then I will
Chapter __)   (tool from Chapter __)
get there.

I will embrace my action animal _____. Their
(animal you most identified with)
strengths are now my strengths.

The journey won't be simple, the rise won't be immediate. But it *will* be exhilarating and most of all worth it. Taking action will be something I *never* regret.

Your Personal Covenant

I, _____, commit to taking action, and no matter what roadblock stands in my way, I will not let it hold me back from achieving my dreams of _____

_____.

I can and I will DO IT!

Sign your personal covenant to make it a CONTRACT with yourself.

_____   _____

(Your Signature)	(Date Signed)

I'll leave you with one last anecdote.

There was a man who wanted to come to America to make a better life for himself and his family.

He diligently saved what he could year after year and finally had enough money to purchase a ticket on a ship to America. He brought a block of cheese and a box of crackers to eat on the trip. He would often go by the dining room and peer in the window at the extravagant meals being served to guests and his stomach would ache with hunger. He longed for the life the other guests enjoyed.

When the ship docked, one of the workers asked him why he never joined them for any meals. The worker asked the man if there was something wrong with the food.

The man replied, "The food looked delicious but I only had enough money for the ticket, not enough for the meals."

The worker told him the meals were all included in the purchase price of the ticket.

"We had your place set at every meal and wondered why you never joined us."

It's time to claim what is rightfully yours. You have the tools and the ability.

Knowing is the first step. Now it's time to start *doing*.

Your future of fulfillment is already set, the table has been prepared.

Don't starve yourself from life's most delectable offerings because you think you deserve cheese and crackers. I promise you have an open invitation to so much more.

Do yourself a favor and pull up a chair. We've been waiting for you. I dare you to ... DO IT!

***

For all resources mentioned in the book and more go to www.davidnurse.com.

You will be able to access a bonus chapter, more tools for taking action, a guide on creating your personal road map, and the potential to work with me personally!

Bibliography

Chapter 1

Grossmann, T. (2013). The role of medial prefrontal cortex in early social cognition. *Frontiers in Human Neuroscience*, 7, 340. https://www.frontiersin.org/articles/10.3389/fnhum.2013.00340/full

Helmenstine, A. M. (2019). Do hippos sweat blood? Chemical composition of hippopotamus blood sweat. ThoughtCo (30 May). https://www.thoughtco.com/do-hippos-sweat-blood-3976013

Howe, J. (1999). He said, she said: Telling tall tales about your partner can improve the way you think about relationships—but worsen your actual memory. *Psychology Today* (1 July). https://www.psychologytoday.com/us/articles/199907/he-said-she-said

Teglasi, H., Caputo, M. H., and Scott, A. L. (2022). Explicit and implicit theory of mind and social competence: A social information processing framework. *New Ideas in Psychology*, 64. https://www.sciencedirect.com/science/article/abs/pii/S0732118X21000647

Chapter 2

Bellis, M. (2020). Biography of Lewis Latimer, noted black inventor. ThoughtCo (8 November). https://www.thoughtco.com/lewis-latimer-profile-1992098

Black Inventor. (n.d.). Lewis Latimer. https://blackinventor.com/lewis-latimer/

Edison Awards. (n.d.). Lewis Latimer. https://edisonawards.com/lewislatimer.php

The Institution of Engineering and Technology. (2020). Lewis Howard Latimer life story: Inventor and innovator. https://www.youtube.com/watch?v=vnehQD9NCrE

Ishler, J. (2021). How to release "emotional baggage" and the tension that goes with it. Healthline (16 September). https://www.healthline.com/health/mind-body/how-to-release-emotional-baggage-and-the-tension-that-goes-with-it#How-do-emotions-get-trapped

Robson, D. (2020). The "Batman effect": How having an alter ego empowers you. BBC: The Life Project (17 August). https://www.bbc.com/worklife/article/20200817-the-batman-effect-how-having-an-alter-ego-empowers-you

Scully, S. (n.d.). Can you get "stuck" at the age you experienced trauma? PsychCentral (4 January). https://psychcentral.com/ptsd/signs-trauma-has-you-stuck#effects-of-trauma

CHAPTER 3

A Mighty Girl Staff. (2022). Sybil Ludington: The 16-year-old revolutionary hero who rode twice as far as Paul Revere. A Mighty Girl (4 April). https://www.amightygirl.com/blog?p=24115#:~:text=On%20the%20night%20of%20April,the%20town%20of%20Danbury%2C%20Connecticut

American Battlefield Trust. (n.d.). Sybil Ludington. https://www.battlefields.org/learn/biographies/sybil-ludington

The Editors of Encyclopaedia Britannica. (2022). Sybil Ludington: American Revolutionary War heroine. *Encyclopaedia Britannica* (30 May). https://www.britannica.com/biography/Sybil-Ludington

Eschner, K. (2017). Was there really a teenage, female Paul Revere? Smithsonianmag.org (26 April). https://www.smithsonianmag.com/smithsonianmag/was-there-really-teenage-female-paul-revere-180962993

Lieberman, C. (2019). Why you procrastinate (it has nothing to do with self-control). *New York Times* (25 March). https://www.nytimes.com/2019/03/25/smarter-living/why-you-procrastinate-it-has-nothing-to-do-with-self-control.html

Murphy, M. (2010). The truth behind procrastination—it's more deadly than you'd think. *Business Insider* (22 October). https://www.businessinsider.com/the-truth-behind-procrastination-its-more-deadly-than-youd-think-2010-10

CHAPTER 4

Blakemore, E. (2018). This athlete conquered poverty, racism, and polio in order to become an Olympian. Timeline (3 May). https://timeline.com/wilma-rudolph-broke-barriers-and-expectations-when-she-won-the-olympics-c3e5de2d412

The Editors of Encyclopaedia Britannica. (2022). Wilma Rudolph. *Encyclopaedia Britannica* (19 June). https://www.britannica.com/biography/Wilma-Rudolph

McLeod, S. (2018). Fundamental attribution error. *Simply Psychology* (31 October).https://www.simplypsychology.org/fundamental-attribution.html

Roberts, M.B. (n.d.). Rudolph ran and the world went wild. ESPN.com. Retrieved September 15, 2022 from https://www.espn.com/sportscentury/features/00016444.html

CHAPTER 5

Rimfield, K., Ayorech, Z., Dale, P. S. et al. (2016). Genetics affects choice of academic subjects as well as achievement. *Scientific Reports*, 6(1), 26373. https://www.researchgate.net/publication/304029247_Genetics_affects_choice_of_academic_subjects_as_well_as_achievement

Terracciano, A., & McCrae, R. R. (2006). Cross-cultural studies of personality traits and their relevance to psychiatry. *Epidemiologia e Psichiatria Sociale*, 15(3), 176–184. https://www.ncbi.nlm.nih.gov/pmc/articles/PMC2756039/

Yerebaken, D. (2021). Barnum effect: The reason why we believe our horoscopes. Neurofied (26 February). https://neurofied.com/barnum-effect-the-reason-why-we-believe-our-horoscopes/

CHAPTER 6

Burns, D. D. (1980). The perfectionist's script for self-defeat. *Psychology Today* (November). https://jessegalef.com/wp-content/uploads/2020/08/the-perfectionist-script-for-self-defeat.pdf

Curran, T. (2018). Perfectionism among young people significantly increased since 1980s, study finds. American Psychology Association (2 January). https://www.apa.org/news/press/releases/2018/01/perfectionism-young-people

CHAPTER 7

Australian Red Cross. (n.d.). James Harrison's story. https://www.lifeblood.com.au/news-and-stories/stories/james-harrison

Cassingham, R. (2020). The man with the golden arm. True Uncommon Sense (15 October). https://medium.com/true-uncommon-sense/the-man-with-the-golden-arm-8a26768a4d71

Castrillion, C. (2019). Why failure leads to career success. Forbes.com (20 November). https://www.forbes.com/sites/carolinecastrillon/2019/11/20/why-failure-leads-to-career-success/?sh=3eeb384b7578

Criss, D. (2018). He donated blood every week for 60 years and saved the lives of 2.4 million babies. CNN Heroes (25 December). https://www.cnn.com/2018/05/11/health/james-harrison-blood-donor-retires-trnd/index.html

Domonoske, C. (2018). Australia's "man with the golden arm" retires after saving 2.4 million babies. The Two-Way (14 May). https://www.npr.org/sections/thetwo-way/2018/05/14/611074956/australias-man-with-the-golden-arm-retires-after-saving-2-4-million-babies

LaFreniere L. S., & Newman M. G. (2020). Exposing worry's deceit: Percentage of untrue worries in generalized anxiety disorder treatment. *Behavior Therapy*, *3*, 413–423. doi: 10.1016/j.beth.2019.07.003

CHAPTER 8

Burkeman, O. (2015). Why are we so distracted all the time? 99U (5 August). https://99u.adobe.com/articles/51300/why-are-we-so-distracted-all-the-time

Klemp, N. (n.d.). Harvard psychologists reveal the real reason we're all so distracted. Inc. https://www.inc.com/nate-klemp/harvard-psychologists-reveal-real-reason-were-all-so-distracted.html

LePrince-Ringuet, D. (2018). Here's scientific proof your brain was designed to be distracted. Wired (22 August). https://www.wired.co.uk/article/brain-distraction-procrastination-science

Trafton, A. (2019). How we tune out distractions. MIT News (12 June). https://news.mit.edu/2019/how-brain-ignores-distractions-0612

Wessel, J. R., Jenkinson, N., Brittain, J.-S., et al. (2016). Surprise disrupts cognition via fronto-basal ganglia suppressive mechanism. *Nature Communication*, *7*, 11195. https://www.nature.com/articles/ncomms11195

CHAPTER 9

Bluerock, G. (2020). The 9 most common regrets people have at the end of life. MBG Mindfulness (24 February). https://www.mindbodygreen.com/0-23024/the-9-most-common-regrets-people-have-at-the-end-of-life.html

Caprino, K. (2019). The top regrets of the dying and what we need to learn from them. Forbes.com (13 December). https://www.forbes.com/sites/kathycaprino/2019/12/13/the-top-regrets-of-the-dying-and-what-we-need-to-learn-from-them/?sh=3ddf07567ce7

Cleveland Clinic. (n.d.). Serotonin. https://my.clevelandclinic.org/health/articles/22572-serotonin

Dartmouth College. (2014). Dartmouth researchers discover a source of self-esteem in the brain. Press release (16 June). https://home.dartmouth.edu/news/2014/06/dartmouth-researchers-discover-source-self-esteem-brain

Lipinski, S. (2021). The biological basis of complacency. *Incident Prevention* (15 April). https://incident-prevention.com/blog/the-biological-basis-of-complacency/#:~:text=Complacency%20is%20a%20byproduct%20of,how%20the%20brain%20is%20designed

Rouault, M., Lebreton, M., & Pessiglione, M. (2021). A shared brain system forming confidence judgment across cognitive domains. bioRxiv (20 September). https://www.researchgate.net/publication/354735819_A_shared_brain_system_forming_confidence_judgment_across_cognitive_domains

University College London. (2017). Self-esteem mapped in the human brain. *ScienceDaily* (24 October). https://www.sciencedaily.com/releases/2017/10/171024103319.htm

ACKNOWLEDGMENTS

God, I never expected I would be writing books and speaking to hundreds of thousands of people for a living. You have far exceeded my wildest dreams and my biggest prayers, but I know the best is *still* yet to come.

Taylor, this book doesn't exist without you. This was your idea, your concept, and you were with me every step of the way during the writing process. There will never be enough words I can write or say that will express my unconditional love for you!

Ann and Dan, aka Mom and Dad, thank you for always supporting me to "go for my dreams" no matter how outrageous they were. You both showed me what it is like to raise a family based on love, support, and God. I am forever grateful! To Sherrill and Ed, aka mother-in-law and father-in-law, thank you for giving me your amazing daughter and for all your support!

Julia, my sister, thank you for being a creative mind working tirelessly with me on this book all while raising a family with three young kids and giving birth to your fourth in the process! Your mastery of the English language is truly an amazing talent.

Paul, my brother, your drive and work ethic is like none I have ever seen before! You have always taken action in your life, hence why you are saving thousands of lives as a doctor today!

The Wiley team. To have publishers who believe in me and genuinely do everything possible to help me succeed—that doesn't happen in this business. I hope you know how much you all mean to me!

Justin D. James and Julie Kerr. Your writing and editing brilliances are big reasons I believe this book is going to touch millions of lives!

The nine incredible people in history outlined in this book: Martha Graham, Lewis Latimer, Sybil Ludington, Wilma Rudolph, Isabel Briggs, Ward Piggy Lambert, James Harrison, Isaac Newton, and John Osteen. Thank you for taking action. Thank you for not giving in to the immense pressure and fear I'm sure you faced. Thank you for committing your life to taking action and benefiting the lives of millions to come!

To everyone who has ever encouraged me to take action. To everyone who has reached out to support me when there was nothing I could give them in return. To everyone who has truly believed in me, I thank you.

To you, right now reading this book, wondering if there is more to life. There is. Trust me, there is. You can do it, keep going and never give up. Take action today and your life of fulfillment is out there waiting for you!

ABOUT THE AUTHOR

David Nurse is the author of the best-selling books *Pivot & Go* and *Breakthrough*. He was named by Real Leaders as one of the Top 50 Motivational Speakers in the World. His podcast, The David Nurse Show, is one of the fastest-growing podcasts on Apple Podcasts and Spotify. David has worked with more than 150 NBA players, top professional sports coaches, CEOs, and Hollywood actors, helping them transform their mindset to succeed at the highest level.

David resides in Marina del Rey, California, with his "much better half"—the gorgeous actress and producer, Taylor Kalupa. The most important thing to David is his relationship with Jesus, spending time with his wife, and, of course, taking their Havamalt puppy Pivot on long walks on the beach.

INDEX